THE FAMILY TREASURY
OF GREAT HOLIDAY IDEAS

THE FAMILY TREASURY
OF GREAT HOLIDAY IDEAS

*Relish, Reflect on, and Remember
the Joys of the Season*

A BARBOUR BOOK

The Family Treasury of Great Holiday Ideas

© 1993 by Barbour and Company, Inc.

ISBN 1-55748-624-7

EVANGELICAL CHRISTIAN PUBLISHERS ASSOCIATION 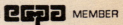 MEMBER

Published by Barbour and Company, Inc.
P.O. Box 719
Uhrichsville, Ohio 44683

Typesetting by Typetronix, Inc., Ft. Myers, Florida

Printed in the United States of America

CONTENTS

INTRODUCTION

Another book on great holiday ideas? you may ask. Why bother?

Picture, if you will, a great construction site. The "pillars" of the holidays are well known to all of us. A Thanksgiving table, laden with a wholesome and delectable bounty; a Christmas tree, bedecked and twinkling, its starry spire tickling the ceiling; the eager faces of little ones, rosy with anticipation at the thought of so many gifts just for them.

The cornerstone of the season, the foundation, is the birth of our Lord, Jesus Christ. Despite the almost irresistible features sustaining the holidays, as Christians we strive to focus on the awesome majesty of His first coming.

But hold on, we're not through! Look closer and you'll see the workers—some intense, some lackadaisical—all trying in their own way to get the job done, some more successfully than others. Picture yourself rushing to find the perfect last-minute gift, baking one more batch of cookies, making a futile effort to hold down the fort despite the rampant commercialism. Or picture yourself depressed or nostalgic, longing for a holiday that once was bright, longing for ways to "get into" the season.

The Family Treasury of Great Holiday Ideas gives you the nuts and bolts to create the holidays of your dreams . . . and the inspiration to build upon and create new traditions of your own. At the same time, you can sit back and enjoy uplifting, sometimes humorous, and always touching musings by some of today's best-known Christian writers. Contributors from all across the United States have generously "invited" us into their homes (and their kitchens!) for everything from the carving of the turkey to the dismantling of the tree . . . and even to a very unusual New Year's Eve party!

So, come relish, reflect on, and remember with us the Joy of the season, and yes, all the other joys that are because of Him as well. May your holidays forever be blessed by those special touches that say this is your home, *this is your family.*

THE FAMILY TREASURY
OF GREAT HOLIDAY IDEAS

Over the river and through the woods
And straight through the barnyard gate.
It seems that we go so dreadfully slow;
It is so hard to wait.
Over the river and through the woods,
Now Grandma's cap I spy.
Hurrah for fun; the pudding's done;
Hurrah for the pumpkin pie.

Traditional

RELISH

A Treasury
of Holiday Recipes

CONTENTS

Festive Beginnings

Merry Salads

Hearty Entrées

Holiday Breads and Seasonal Accompaniments

Sweet Endings

The Family Treasury of Great Holiday Ideas

Welcome to My Home

SHRIMP DIP

One 8-ounce package cream cheese
½ cup mayonnaise
1 cup chopped shrimp (boiled)
½ teaspoon Worcestershire sauce
¼ teaspoon garlic
1 bunch green onions, chopped
¼ teaspoon celery salt

Let the cream cheese stand at room temperature until soft. Mix all of the above ingredients together. Serve with crackers, or whatever you prefer.

Linda Duhan
resides in
Lafayette, Louisiana.

QUICK ONION DIP

1 pint sour cream
1¼-ounce package dehydrated onion soup mix
Chopped pimientos
Chopped green or black olives
Chopped mushrooms
4 tablespoons finely chopped English walnuts (optional)

Blend together sour cream (or imitation) and dehydrated onion-soup mix. Add pimientos, green or black olives, or mushrooms, according to taste. All should be well drained before adding to dip. For variety, add English walnuts. Keeps well up to one week in refrigerator. Store covered.

Taken from: THE JUNE MASTERS BACHER COUNTRY COOKBOOK *by June Masters Bacher. Copyright © 1988 by Harvest House Publishers, Eugene, Oregon 97402. Used by permission.*

CALIFORNIA GOLD DIP

½ cup sour cream
½ cup mayonnaise
1 teaspoon Worcestershire sauce
½ teaspoon prepared mustard
½ teaspoon curry powder
2 tablespoons chopped chives
½ cup chopped black olives

Blend sour cream with mayonnaise. Add remaining ingredients, folding in olives and chives last. Refrigerate. Keeps well for a week.

GUACAMOLE

4 ripe avocados (peeled, seeded, chopped)
½ cup mayonnaise
¼ cup dry onion (peeled, chopped)
3 tablespoons lime or lemon juice
2 teaspoons chili powder and 1 teaspoon salt, blended
1 teaspoon garlic powder (or 1 clove, chopped)
½ teaspoon Tabasco sauce
2 medium tomatoes (peeled, diced)

Mash avocados with fork or purée in blender. Mix remaining ingredients except tomatoes. May be prepared a day in advance. In order to retain color, push at least one avocado seed into dip and cover bowl tightly with plastic wrap. When ready to serve, remove avocado seed, garnish dip with tomatoes, and sprinkle with paprika.

Taken from: THE JUNE MASTERS BACHER COUNTRY COOKBOOK
*by June Masters Bacher. Copyright © 1988 by Harvest House Publishers,
Eugene, Oregon 97402. Used by permission.*

R E L I S H

BEAN DIP SUPREME

1 can (16 ounces) refried beans
4 ounces green chilies
4 ounces taco sauce or salsa
1½ cups shredded Cheddar or Monterey jack cheese
3 ounces black olives
4 ounces sour cream

Chop green chilies and black olives. Spread refried beans across bottom of shallow 9-inch ovenproof dish. Follow with a layer of chilies and a layer of taco sauce. Cover with cheese. Bake at 350°F until bubbly (about 20 minutes). Top with black olives and dollops of sour cream. Serve with tortilla chips.

Therese Hoehlein Cerbie
resides in
Harrington Park, New Jersey.

FRESH SALSA

1 tablespoon whole coriander seeds
5 ripe tomatoes
1 bunch scallions
2 small cans green chopped chilies
1 tablespoon each: hot water, salt, sugar, red wine vinegar,
    olive oil
Tabasco sauce or Louisiana hot sauce to taste

Crush whole coriander seeds and add hot water. Let sit. Chop tomatoes and scallions, including tops. Add green chilies and mix. Add sugar, salt, vinegar, and olive oil. Add drained hot water "juice" from coriander seeds to salsa mixture. Add Tabasco to taste, about 5 to 10 shakes. Makes enough for 2 bags of tortilla chips!

Ellen Caughey
resides in
Harrington Park, New Jersey.

The Family Treasury of Great Holiday Ideas

CHEESE STRAWS

2 cups all-purpose flour
1¾ cups sharp cheese, grated
⅔ cup butter
Dash of red pepper
3 tablespoons cold water

Cut butter into flour with pastry cutter. Stir in cheese and pepper. Sprinkle with water. Stir with fork and work into dough. Roll out on floured board. Cut into narrow strips with fluted pastry wheel, about 3 inches long. Bake at 350°F for about 10 minutes. Makes about 150. Sprinkle with grated Parmesan cheese before baking. Place carefully in a box with waxed paper between each layer and give as gifts.

KITCHEN POTPOURRI

1 cup dried lemon peel
1 cup dried orange peel
1 cup whole cloves
12 cinnamon sticks, broken into 2-inch pieces
½ cup whole allspice

A heaping spoonful of this mixture simmering in an open pan of water on the back of the stove will fill your home with a spicy aroma. May be stored in refrigerator and used again and again. Put in small decorative jars and give as gifts!

June Blackford
resides in
Nicholasville, Kentucky.

R E L I S H

Two small cans of chicken
8 ounces cream cheese
⅓ cup diced celery
¼ cup chopped parsley
2 teaspoons A-1 Steak Sauce
1 teaspoon curry powder

Mix together and refrigerate 4 to 12 hours. Just before serving take the chicken out and roll it into a log shape. Mix a cup of chopped walnuts and a cup of chopped parsley together on a cookie sheet and roll the log in the mixture so that parsley and nuts cover the outside. Serve on a plate with small crackers all around. Provide a knife so people can serve themselves bite-size portions on bite-size crackers.

Stormie Omartian
is a best-selling author, singer, and fitness
expert. Her books include
A Step in the Right Direction
(Thomas Nelson) and her autobiography,
Stormie *(Harvest House Publishers).*

Spiced oranges: Stud 3 oranges with whole cloves, ½ inch apart. Place in baking pan with a little water and bake slowly for 30 minutes at 325°F.

Wassail: 3 quarts apple cider
Two 3-inch cinnamon sticks
½ teaspoon nutmeg
½ cup honey
⅓ cup lemon juice
2 teaspoons lemon rind
5 cups pineapple juice

Heat cider and cinnamon sticks in large saucepan. Bring to boil. Simmer, covered, 5 minutes. Add remaining ingredients and simmer, uncovered, 5 minutes longer. Pour into punch bowl and float spiced oranges on top, using cinnamon sticks for stirring or put into crockpot on high to keep hot. Makes 40 cups.

Kathleen Yapp
is a versatile and prolific writer who resides
in Gainesville, Georgia. Among her
inspirational romances
is A New Song *(Heartsong Presents).*

CLARA'S BEST CRANBERRY SALAD

1 pound fresh cranberries
Rind of one orange, grated
1 small can crushed pineapple
1½ cups sugar
1 cup crushed pecans (optional)
1 large box any kind of red Jell-O
1 cup boiling water
1 package plain gelatin
½ cup cold water
1 large package cream cheese

Dissolve the Jell-O. Dissolve the plain gelatin in ½ cup cold water. Put in blender or food processor. Add fresh cranberries until well crushed. Add the cream cheese and sugar. Pour into a large bowl and add all other ingredients. Let chill and serve. Serves eight people easily.

Linda Herring
*is a first grade teacher as well as
a published writer of inspirational romance.
Among her books is* Yesterday's Tomorrows
*(Heartsong Presents).
She resides in Monahans, Texas.*

COLLEEN'S BRING-TO-FAMILY-DINNER FRUIT SALAD

4 large oranges (roll before peeling to loosen skin and release juice)

4 large bananas (cut at last minute, although rest of salad can be made ahead of time)

1 large can pineapple tidbits, well drained

Maraschino cherries, to taste (save some for decorating top)

1 pint whipping cream (forget the cholesterol for once; although a whipped topping can be substituted, it won't be as good)

Whip cream, add well-drained fruit, make cherry design on top. Makes a *large* bowlful.

Variations: Add fresh strawberries, marshmallows, and so on. For holidays, I add a drop of red or green food coloring and tint the whipped cream pale green or pink.

COLLEEN'S TASTES-LIKE-MORE POTATO SALAD

4 medium potatoes, cooked and cooled to handling temperature (best to use White Rose potatoes)

1 medium onion (better yet, several green onions with tops), chopped fine

4 hard-boiled eggs, cooled and chopped

4 dill pickles, chopped fine

Toss lightly with a prestirred blend of mayonnaise, prepared mustard, and a little dill pickle juice and pepper. Good served right away or chilled. Either use right away or put in refrigerator until needed.

Variations: Black or ripe olives, cherry tomatoes, and/or fresh parsley can be used for garnish.

Colleen L. Reece
is one of the most beloved writers of Christian romance. She resides in Auburn, Washington.

R E L I S H

CHRISTMAS FRUIT SALAD

This fruit salad was a favorite in the Morris household, so when I married a Morris forty-four years ago, I had to carry on this tradition.

2 large cans fruit cocktail
4 or 5 bananas, sliced
1 cup pecans, chopped
2 tablespoons Miracle Whip

Mix fruit cocktail, bananas, and pecans together. Chill in refrigerator overnight. Add Miracle Whip the next day and mix in well. Serves 8 to 10. This makes a good dessert with white cake.

Johnnie Morris
is married to Gilbert Morris, best-selling
Christian author (with Bobby Funderburk) of
A Call to Honor *and* The Color of the Star
(Word Publishers).
The Morrises reside in
Baton Rouge, Louisiana.

CRANBERRY RELISH

I like to make Cranberry Relish at Thanksgiving and then freeze half of the relish for the busy Christmas season.

4 medium oranges, seeded
2 pounds cranberries
4 medium unpeeled apples, cored
4 cups sugar

Take the yellow peel from oranges; trim off and discard white part. Put orange pulp and yellow peel, cranberries, and apples through food chopper. Add sugar and mix well. Makes 4 pints.

Irene Burkholder
resides in
Leola, Pennsylvania.

The Family Treasury of Great Holiday Ideas

Because other family members are so far away, Christmas means sharing through packages. I have found that I can share a part of my bountiful Alaskan harvest by adding a jar of jam to each box sent. This gives a treat from Alaska and adds a little sparkle to the festivities.

2 oranges	4 cups lowbush cranberries
1 lemon	6½ cups sugar
⅛ teaspoon baking soda	3 ounces liquid pectin
1¾ cups water	

Remove seeds from the oranges and lemon and cut fruit into large pieces. Do not remove peel. Grind fruit. Add the baking soda and water. Cover and simmer 20 minutes, stirring occasionally. Add berries and continue simmering, covered, for 10 minutes. Measure exactly 5 cups of prepared fruit into a large saucepan, add sugar. Bring to full, rolling boil for 1 minute. Remove from heat and stir in pectin. Skim and stir for 5 minutes, allowing marmalade to cool slightly. Ladle into hot, sterilized, canning jars and seal with lids. Process for 15 minutes in a boiling water bath.

Joyce Turner
resides in
McGrath, Alaska.

FAVORITE HOLIDAY FRUIT SALAD

1 can peach pie filling
1 no. 2 can pineapple tidbits (drained)
One 11-ounce can mandarin orange slices (drained)
1 box frozen strawberries (thawed and drained)

Mix above at last minute, cut 1 large banana, pour ½ cup lemon juice over it, and drain. Add to above and chill.
   Optional: ½ cup blueberries or 1 can drained fruit cocktail can be added.

Bessie R. Fortenberry
resides in
Brandon, Mississippi.

CRANBERRY JELLO

6-ounce package cherry Jell-O (1 large or 2 small packages)
2 cups boiling water
1 can whole cranberry sauce
1 16-ounce container sour cream
¼ cup chopped walnuts

Mix Jell-O with boiling water; stir until dissolved. Stir in canned cranberries and pour into wreath-shaped mold. Chill until thickened (about 1 hour). Stir in sour cream and nuts. Chill until firm. Remove from mold and serve.
   Holiday note: For Christmas, empty a box of green Jell-O into small mixing bowl and prepare according to directions on box. When firm take a knife and slide along side of bowl and ease into center of cranberry Jell-O wreath. Top with whipped cream if desired.

JoAnn Otto
resides in
Cortland, New York.

The Family Treasury of Great Holiday Ideas

ROAST BEEF TENDERLOIN

One 6-pound whole beef tenderloin	Kitchen Bouquet
1 clove garlic	Freshly ground pepper

About 1¼ hours before serving, preheat oven to 450°F. Remove any surface fat and connective tissue from tenderloin. Rub surface with garlic and Kitchen Bouquet. Press fresh pepper in meat.

Place on wire rack in shallow open pan, tucking narrow end under to make roast more uniformly thick. Insert meat thermometer into center at thickest part. Roast about 60 minutes or until thermometer reads 140°F. Meat is crusty brown outside, pink to red inside.

Cut tenderloin into 1-inch-thick slices; arrange on heated platter. Spoon BÉARNAISE SAUCE over slices or serve it from gravy boat. Makes 8 to 10 servings.

BÉARNAISE SAUCE

3 shallots or little green onions, chopped fine	½ cup butter, softened
1 teaspoon dried tarragon	½ teaspoon salt
¼ cup wine vinegar	Dash of Tabasco sauce
¼ cup white vinegar	2 teaspoons chopped parsley
1 tablespoon lemon juice	3 egg yolks

Bring to boil in saucepan shallots, tarragon, and both vinegars. Boil until sauce becomes glaze. In heavy saucepan, mix egg yolks and lemon juice with wire whisk. Over low heat or hot water, beat in butter, 1 tablespoon at a time, until thickened. Stir in glaze and rest of ingredients. Serve warm with roast beef.

Marabel Morgan
is the author of The Total Woman *(Revell)*
and other best-sellers. She resides
in Miami, Florida.

Taken from: Marabel Morgan, *The Total Woman Cookbook*, Fleming H. Revell, a division of Baker Book House Company, Copyright © 1980.

RELISH

CHEESE GRITS SOUFFLÉ
Also called Georgia Ice Cream

1½ cups quick grits
2 teaspoons salt
6 cups boiling water
1 pound grated Cheddar
   cheese
3 eggs, beaten

Dash of Tabasco sauce
1½ sticks butter, melted
1 tablespoon seasoned salt
⅛ teaspoon paprika
1 teaspoon Worcestershire
   sauce

Cook grits and salt in water for 5 minutes. (If regular grits are used, cook 20 minutes.) Mix all ingredients and pour into well-greased 3-quart casserole. May be refrigerated overnight. Bake 1 hour at 350°F or 2½ hours at 275°F. Serves 8.

Marabel Morgan
is the author of The Total Woman *(Revell)*
and other best-sellers. She resides
in Miami, Florida.

Taken from: Marabel Morgan, *The Total Woman Cookbook*, Fleming H. Revell, a division of Baker Book House Company, Copyright © 1980.

CHRISTMAS BEEF BARBECUE

One 3-pound roast beef, baked tender
1 bottle (regular size) catsup
2 shakes Tabasco sauce
Horseradish per individual taste, (optional)

After beef roast has cooled, shred apart in a large bowl. In a small bowl mix catsup, horseradish, and Tabasco sauce. Combine catsup mixture with meat and cover until ready to use. When ready, warm mixture and serve on large buns.

Margaret Layton Hunt
resides in
Charlotte, North Carolina.

The Family Treasury of Great Holiday Ideas

CABBAGE ROLLS

½ pound hamburger (uncooked)
½ cup ham (cut fine)
1 small onion
1 cup rice
Salt and pepper to taste

Mix all together. Roll in cabbage leaves and place in baking dish. Add some water and bake in 375°F oven until rice is tender (approximately 1 hour). (If you put cabbage in boiling salted water and boil about 2 minutes and drain the leaves, they can be pulled apart easily.)

KRAUT BEROK

1 medium head cabbage
Salt and pepper to taste
3 large onions
2 pounds hamburger

Fry hamburger in large skillet until it begins to brown. Add chopped onions and cabbage. Add salt and pepper to taste and fry until cabbage is done.

*Alice Schenk
resides in
Rupert, Idaho.*

Around Christmas in Baton Rouge, Louisiana, there's finally a bit of chill in the air—most times. There's nothing like a big pot of warm soup on the stove when the children and husband come in from the cold. This recipe, handed down by my mother, is the favorite of my three teenage sons. (The oldest is going out of state to college this year, and he's already asked if there's some way I could send him some minestrone in the mail.)

¾ to 1 pound ham, cut in cubes
Small onion, diced
2 tablespoons minced parsley (optional)
1 clove minced garlic, or ⅛ teaspoon garlic powder
1 cup shredded cabbage
½ cup diced celery
Salt and pepper to taste

9 cups water
1 cup diced potatoes
½ cup diced carrots
1 tablespoon oil
1 cup dried lima beans, soaked overnight
8 beef bouillon cubes
1 cup fresh or canned tomatoes
½ cup macaroni or spaghetti (broken in pieces)

Sauté celery, minced garlic, and onion lightly in oil. Drain on paper towel. Return to covered pot and simmer everything but the macaroni 1½ hours. Add macaroni, salt and pepper (may not need any salt, because the ham and bouillon cubes are salty), simmer 30 more minutes.

If you don't get a chance to soak the lima beans overnight, put them in a small pot with about three cups of water (subtract from the 9 cups that you need). Bring to boil, cover, and remove from heat. Let sit for an hour, then pour beans and water into other soup ingredients before starting to cook.

Kate Blackwell
*is a new and promising writer of
inspirational romance. She is the author of*
Shores of Promise *(Heartsong Presents).*

FESTIVE WAIKIKI MEATBALLS

1½ pounds ground beef
⅔ cup cracker crumbs
½ cup coarsely chopped red onion
1 egg
1½ teaspoons salt
¼ teaspoon ginger
¼ cup milk
½ teaspoon garlic salt
¾ cup red pepper, chopped
¾ cup green bell pepper, chopped
½ cup shredded coconut
2 cups water
2 tablespoons cornstarch
¾ cup brown sugar
1 can (13 ounces) pineapple chunks (save juice)
½ cup vinegar
4 tablespoons soy sauce
1 small package slivered almonds
1 small can water chestnuts (drained)

Mix beef, crumbs, onion, egg, salt, ginger, milk, and garlic salt and shape into balls. Brown in skillet, pour off fat.

Mix water, brown sugar, juice from pineapple, vinegar, and soy sauce and bring to a rapid boil. Add cornstarch and mix until thickened (stirring constantly). Pour over meatballs that have been placed in baking dish or dutch oven. Place peppers, pineapple, coconut, almonds, and chestnuts around meatballs and bake at 300°F for 45 minutes or in a slow cooker on low for several hours.

Can be served on toothpicks as finger foods or over rice for a delicious meal.

Judy Boen
resides in
Bakersfield, California.

RELISH

2 cups diced turkey
1 cup celery (sliced diagonally)
¼ cup dry roasted peanuts
⅔ cup mayonnaise
2 tablespoons lime juice
½ teaspoon curry powder
1 cup drained pineapple chunks
½ cup sliced green onion
1 cup seedless green grapes
2 tablespoons chopped chutney
½ teaspoon grated lime rind
¼ teaspoon salt

Toss together the first six ingredients. Combine remaining ingredients to make a dressing. Stir dressing into turkey mixture. Serve on a bed of greens. May be doubled or tripled.

Taken from: THE JUNE MASTERS BACHER COUNTRY COOKBOOK
*by June Masters Bacher. Copyright © 1988 by Harvest House Publishers,
Eugene, Oregon 97402. Used by permission.*

JULEKAGE

My husband Jan and I are of Scandinavian heritage and thus many of the Christmas foods served in our home are of Scandinavian origin. One of our favorites is Julekage or Julekake, a Christmas bread. The following recipe for Julekage was handed on by my mother-in-law. Jan and I especially enjoy this bread toasted and spread with butter.

Whether celebrating in North Carolina or with our large families in Minnesota, a Swedish saying rings in our hearts at the end of Christmas Eve and Christmas Day, as we celebrate Christ's birth. Takk for i dag . . . Thanks for the day.

2 cakes or packages of yeast	1 teaspoon salt
1 cup milk	6 cardamom seeds, ground
(¾ cup milk and ¼ cup water if dry yeast is used instead of cake yeast)	4 cups flour
	⅛ pound butter
	⅔ package candied fruit
½ cup sugar	Black raisins
2 eggs	White raisins

Scald and cool milk. When milk is lukewarm, dissolve yeast in milk. Mix in sugar, slightly beaten egg, salt, cardamom, and 2 cups of flour. Melt butter and add to mixture. Mix well. Add remaining flour, but keep dough sticky. Mix in candied fruit and a good handful each of black and white raisins, packing in as much fruit as the mixture will hold. Knead on floured board until smooth. Put into a greased bowl to rise. (Dough should rise to twice its original size. Due to the fruit, this can take 2 hours or longer.)

After dough has risen, cut dough down with a knife while still in bowl, instead of punching or kneading. Let rise again, about 45 minutes. Divide dough into two parts and pound down. Shape into loaves and let rise to about twice its size again. Bread can be baked in bread pans, or formed into round loaves and baked on a greased cookie sheet or in a greased pie pan. Bake 30 to 40 minutes at 350°F.

(continued on next page)

RELISH

(continued from previous page)

Bread may be frosted with a powdered sugar frosting while warm.

Frosting:

3 cups powdered sugar   1½ teaspoons almond flavoring
⅓ cup soft butter   2 tablespoons milk

Cream together sugar and butter. Stir in flavoring. Add milk until reach desired consistency.

JoAnn A. Grote
*is the author of the popular inspirational
romance,* The Sure Promise
*(Heartsong Presents). She resides in
Winston-Salem, North Carolina.*

Danish Ebleskiver

This recipe is from my dad's side of the family. My grandmother makes this in a special kind of pan which can be purchased at any international foods shop.

2 cups buttermilk   1 teaspoon salt
2 cups flour   1 teaspoon baking soda
3 eggs   2 teaspoons sugar
1 teaspoon baking powder

Beat egg yolks. Add sugar, salt, and milk. Sift together flour, baking soda, and baking powder and add. Fold in stiffly beaten egg whites. Place small amount fat in each cup of pan and fill ⅓ full of dough. Cook until bubbly. Turn carefully with fork and finish baking on other side. Serve with butter and maple syrup or jam. Also, various fruits are good on these.

Marcee Ekstrum
*resides in
Sioux Falls, South Dakota.*

The Family Treasury of Great Holiday Ideas

PANDESAL
(Favorite breakfast rolls from the Philippines)

A. 2 tablespoons yeast (2 envelopes)
   1 teaspoon white sugar
   1 cup warm water

Mix and let rise.

B. 8 cups all-purpose flour
   1½ cups white sugar

Mix; set aside.

C. 4 eggs
   2 tablespoons vegetable oil
   1 cup warm water
   ¼ cup oil for kneading (optional)

Mix thoroughly.

Mix A and C ingredients together, then add B dry ingredients. Knead mixture. Lay kneaded dough flat on the counter, cut into rolls on bread crumbs, and put rolls on cookie sheets. Let rolls rise for 3 to 4 hours. Bake at 300°F for 15 to 20 minutes, until lightly brown. (These rolls can be frozen after baking. Thaw in warm conventional oven, not microwave.) Serve with butter or margarine or cheese. Enjoy God's many blessings!

Gail McKusick
resides in
Globe, Arizona.

R E L I S H

Our family's all-time favorite bread made its debut one holiday season when I planned Christmas Eve dinner. Needing a hot, crusty bread to complement a rich beef stew and lettuce salad, I played around and came up with this recipe, named for the occasion. The meal was memorable, served on creamy white pottery with the good silver, set on a chocolate brown tablecloth, accompanied by a festive centerpiece of candles and greenery.

That was one of those dream years when I managed to actually put the hubbub of gift wrapping and housecleaning behind me by late afternoon. With this mostly fix-ahead menu, we and our guests enjoyed a leisurely dinner and arrived at the Christmas Eve service in time to get a seat.

Christmas Eve Bread has retained its name, but its popularity has blossomed, making it a year-round treat.

½ cup butter or margarine, softened
¾ cup mayonnaise
1 tablespoon minced chives or finely grated onion
1 tablespoon dried parsley
½ teaspoon oregano
½ teaspoon Worcestershire sauce
¾ cup grated Parmesan cheese
1 loaf french bread
Paprika

Cream together first seven ingredients. Let stand at room temperature one hour.

Cut bread in half lengthwise. Then slice each half into 1-inch slices, working from the cut edge almost through the crust.

Spread butter mixture on top of both halves. Sprinkle with paprika.

Place halves, buttered side down, on shiny side of large sheet of foil. Bring foil over top and seal in a package. Broil five minutes in broiler, buttered side up. Or, bake package fifteen minutes at 400°F.

Mary Carpenter Reid
is a prolific author of fiction, mystery, and romance. Among her books is Rebar *(Heartsong Presents).*
She resides in Brea, California.

CARROT-PINEAPPLE LOAVES

3 cups flour
1 teaspoon baking soda
1 teaspoon salt
1 teaspoon ground ginger
½ teaspoon baking powder
3 large eggs

1 cup vegetable oil
1½ cups sugar
2 cups shredded carrots
1 can (8 ounces) crushed pine-
    apple (drained)
1 cup chopped pecans

Stir together flour, baking soda, salt, ginger, and baking powder. In large bowl at medium speed, beat eggs and oil until well blended. Add sugar and continue beating until mixture is thick, about 2 minutes. On low speed, beat in carrots and pineapple. Add flour mixture and stir until flour is moistened. Stir in nuts. Spoon batter into loaf pans. Bake at 350°F 50 minutes or until toothpick comes out clean. Cool 10 minutes before removing from pans. Makes 4 small loaves.

Patricia Vetense
resides in
Palmyra, Wisconsin.

CRANBERRY NUT BREAD

⅓ cup margarine
1¼ cups sugar
2 eggs
3 cups flour
1 tablespoon baking powder

1 teaspoon salt
½ teaspoon baking soda
¾ cup water
⅓ cup orange juice
1½ cups chopped cranberries

Cream margarine and sugar. Add eggs one at a time. Mix well. Add combined dry ingredients, alternating with water and orange juice. Fold in berries. Pour in greased loaf pan. Bake at 350°F for 1 hour 15 minutes. Cool 15 minutes and remove from pan.
    Especially delicious when toasted, buttered, and eaten warm!

Christine Beckett
resides in Matawan, New Jersey.

RELISH

NEW YEAR'S BAK

1 cup milk	4 packages dry yeast
1 cup sugar	1 cup warm water
2 teaspoons salt	4 eggs
1 cup butter	1 cup raisins
8 cups flour	

Heat milk in saucepan. Remove from heat and add sugar, salt, and butter. Stir until butter is melted. Cool to lukewarm. Sprinkle yeast over water and stir until dissolved. Add milk mixture, eggs, and 4 cups flour. Beat until smooth. Add raisins; with spoon beat in remaining flour. Dough will be soft. Let rise in warm place until doubles in bulk, about 1 hour. Punch down. Knead to smooth. Roll to ½ inch and cut in various shapes. Let rise about 45 minutes. Fry in deep fat at 375°F until brown.

Marcee Ekstrum
resides in
Sioux Falls, South Dakota.

MASHED POTATO ROLLS

1 yeast cake	1 cup milk, scalded
2 eggs	½ cup sugar
1 teaspoon salt	⅔ cup margarine, melted
1 cup leftover cold mashed potatoes	5 cups flour

Add yeast to milk (cooled slightly). Beat in eggs. Add sugar, salt, and margarine. Add potatoes and mix. Sift in 4½ cups flour, reserving ½ cup for kneading. Knead lightly only until mixed, using the ½ cup of reserved flour to dust hands and kneading surface and reduce stickiness of dough. Shape into a ball and let rise in large bowl in warm place 2 hours. Shape into rolls and bake at 400°F for 15 minutes.

Taken from: THE JUNE MASTERS BACHER COUNTRY COOKBOOK
by June Masters Bacher. Copyright © 1988 by Harvest House Publishers,
Eugene, Oregon 97402. Used by permission.

The Family Treasury of Great Holiday Ideas

TREASURE JEWEL BANANA BREAD

1 cup dark brown sugar
2 eggs
½ teaspoon lemon rind
2 cups flour
½ teaspoon cinnamon
1 cup chopped nuts
¼ cup candied cherries

½ cup butter
1 tablespoon lemon juice
1½ cups mashed bananas
1 teaspoon baking soda
½ teaspoon salt
½ cup chocolate chips

Cream sugar and butter. Add eggs, one at a time. Stir in the lemon juice, lemon rind, and bananas. Sift flour, soda, cinnamon, and salt and mix with the creamed mixture. Fold in the nuts, chocolate chips, and cherries. Pour into 9 x 5 x 3-inch pan. Bake at 350°F for 55 minutes or until done.

Judy Boen
resides in
Bakersfield, California.

BUTTER BEANS AU GRATIN

Two 10-ounce packages frozen
    butter beans
3 tablespoons flour
½ teaspoon salt
¼ teaspoon white pepper
¼ cup dry onion, grated

½ teaspoon Worcestershire sauce
½ cup jack cheese, grated
1 tablespoon butter or margarine
2 cups cottage cheese
2 teaspoons sugar

Cook beans as directed. Drain. Mix and stir in flour and 1 cup cottage cheese. Add salt, pepper, Worcestershire, sugar, and onion; mix well. Fold in remaining cottage cheese. Sprinkle jack cheese on top, dot with butter, and bake uncovered at 350°F for 30 minutes or until golden good!

Taken from: THE JUNE MASTERS BACHER COUNTRY COOKBOOK
by June Masters Bacher. Copyright © 1988 by Harvest House Publishers,
Eugene, Oregon 97402. Used by permission.

RELISH

Christmas fare in New Orleans is often centered around seafood. This has been a tradition in the Funderburk household for many years.

2 boxes Chicken Stove Top Stuffing
½ cup chopped green pepper
⅔ cup chopped green onions (include tops)
2½ cups turkey broth (from neck and giblets)
½ cup grated Parmesan cheese
Neck meat and giblets, chopped
1 can mushroom stems and pieces
2 dozen raw oysters (reserve liquid)
5 tablespoons margarine
1 cup chopped celery
4 cloves garlic, minced
1 teaspoon black pepper
2 teaspoons salt
1 egg

Cool broth and pour over dressing mix. Let stand until liquid is absorbed. Sauté celery, onion, green pepper, and garlic in margarine about 5 minutes. Season with salt and pepper. Add cheese and mushrooms, then quartered oysters and cook 5 minutes longer. Combine oyster mixture with dressing mix. Add oyster liquid, giblets, and neck meat and egg. Mix thoroughly.

Makes approximately 7 cups, enough to stuff 12- to 13-pound turkey.

Helen Funderburk
is married to Bobby Funderburk,
coauthor (with Gilbert Morris) of
A Call to Honor *and* The Color of the Star
(Word Publishers).
The Funderburks reside in
Baton Rouge, Louisiana.

The Family Treasury of Great Holiday Ideas

cups crumbled cornbread (made with 3 to 4 eggs)
cups crumbled biscuits or loaf bread
cup chopped green onions
cup chopped celery
hard-boiled eggs (chopped)
stick margarine
apple (peeled and chopped)
salt, pepper, and poultry seasoning (as desired)

Mix above ingredients.

Heat:
can cream of chicken soup
can chicken or turkey broth

Pour over bread mixture and mix well. (Works best if you use your hands!) Bake at 350°F for 45 minutes.

Jane Richardson Holden
resides in
Marion, Mississippi.

CRUNCHY SWEET POTATO CASSEROLE

2 cups mashed sweet potatoes
1¼ cups sugar
2 eggs, beaten
½ cup milk

6 tablespoons melted
    margarine
½ teaspoon cinnamon
½ teaspoon nutmeg

Combine all ingredients above and mix well. Spoon int
greased 2-quart casserole and bake 20 minutes at 400°F
Sprinkle with following topping and bake 10 more minutes.

Topping:

¾ cup crushed wheat cereal
½ cup firmly packed brown sugar
½ cup pecans
6 tablespoons melted margarine
2 teaspoons maple flavoring

SOUTHERN BISCUITS

2 cups all-purpose flour
2 teaspoons sugar
2 teaspoons baking powder
1 teaspoon salt

½ teaspoon baking soda
⅓ cup shortening
⅔ cup buttermilk

Heat over to 450°F. Measure flour, sugar, baking powder, salt
and baking soda into bowl. Cut in shortening thoroughly unti
mixture looks like meal.

Stir in almost all the buttermilk. If dough is not pliable
adjust enough milk to make a soft, puffy, easy-to-roll dough.

Round up dough on lightly floured cloth-covered board
Knead lightly 20 to 25 times, about ½ minute. Roll out ½-inch
thick and cut with floured biscuit cutter. Place on ungreased
baking sheet. Bake for 10 to 12 minutes or until golden brown
Makes about two dozen 1¾-inch biscuits.

*Paula Brann
resides in
Callao, Virginia.*

The Family Treasury of Great Holiday Ideas

BUTTERNUT SQUASH

3 pounds butternut squash
3 tablespoons butter
1 tablespoon + 2 teaspoons
   brown sugar

¼ teaspoon salt
¼ cup light raisins
1 tablespoon light corn syrup
1 tablespoon chopped pecans

Cut butternut squash in half and remove seeds. Bake cut side down in 400°F oven for 45 minutes or until tender. Scoop out pulp and mix with 2 tablespoons butter, 2 teaspoons brown sugar, salt, raisins, and pecans. Turn mixture into casserole. Combine 1 tablespoon butter, 1 tablespoon brown sugar, and light corn syrup and drizzle over squash. Sprinkle with more chopped pecans. Bake at 350°F for 25 minutes. Serves 4 to 6.

GREEN BEAN CASSEROLE

1 can french-style green beans,
   drained
1 can corn, drained
½ cup chopped onion
¼ cup green pepper, chopped
1 cup Cheddar cheese

½ pint sour cream
1 can cream of mushroom
   soup
1 roll Ritz crackers
1 stick butter

Mix first 7 ingredients in a 9 x 12-inch pan. Melt butter and crumble in crackers. Spread on top of vegetable mixture. Bake at 350°F for 45 minutes.

Ellen Nelson
resides in
Cresskill, New Jersey.

2 cups long-grain rice, uncooked
2½ tablespoons beef-flavored bouillon granules
2½ tablespoons parsley flakes
1 tablespoon dried onion flakes
2 teaspoons dried whole basil
1 teaspoon dried whole thyme
½ teaspoon garlic powder

Divide rice and bouillon granules into four gift packages; se
aside. Combine remaining ingredients; stir and divide amon;
gift packages. Seal. Include the following recipe with the pack
ages. Yield: 4 packages.

HERB RICE

1 package herb-rice mix
2½ cups hot water

Combine ingredients in a 1½-quart casserole. Cover and bake a
350°F for 45 minutes or until liquid is absorbed and rice i
tender.

*June Blackford
resides in
Nicholasville, Kentucky.*

2 cups mashed cooked winter squash or one 12-ounce package
  cooked winter squash, thawed
3 tablespoons sugar
1 tablespoon finely chopped onion
¼ teaspoon salt
⅛ teaspoon pepper
4½ cups all-purpose flour
⅔ cup sugar
1 teaspoon baking powder
¼ teaspoon salt
1 cup milk
2 beaten eggs
⅓ cup half and half or light cream
Milk
Sifted powdered sugar (optional)

For filling, in a medium saucepan combine the squash, 3 table-spoons sugar, onion, ¼ teaspoon salt, and pepper. Bring to boiling; reduce heat. Simmer, uncovered, about 15 minutes or until thickened, stirring occasionally. Cool slightly.

Meanwhile, in a large mixing bowl, stir together the flour, ⅓ cup sugar, baking powder, and ¼ teaspoon salt.

In another bowl, stir together the milk, eggs, and cream. Add to dry ingredients and stir just until dough clings together.

On a well-floured surface knead dough gently for 10 to 12 strokes. Roll dough to ¼-inch thickness. (If necessary, chill dough until easy to handle.) Cut into rounds using a 4-inch cutter, dipping cutter into flour between cuts.

Spoon about 1 tablespoon filling onto each round. Fold dough over filling and seal by pinching or pressing with the tines of a fork. Place on a greased baking sheet. Brush tips with milk. Bake in a 375°F oven for 18 minutes or until golden. Sprinkle with sifted powdered sugar, if desired. Serve warm. Makes 12.

Alice Schenk
resides in
Rupert, Idaho.

RELISH

MINCEMEAT SURPRISE COOKIES

1 cup solid vegetable shortening
1 teaspoon salt
1 teaspoon vanilla
1 cup brown sugar, firmly packed
2 eggs, well beaten

1⅔ cup sifted flour
¾ teaspoon baking soda
2 cups (quick) rolled oats
2 cups mincemeat (I use jar or one package of dry mincemeat)

Cream together shortening, salt, vanilla, and brown sugar. Add eggs and blend. Sift flour and baking soda and blend. Add rolled oats and mix thoroughly. Dough is very soft.

Roll dough ⅛-inch thick on floured board. Cut rounds with a 2½-inch cookie cutter. Place 1 heaping teaspoon mincemeat on half the rounds and top with other half. Seal edges together carefully with a fork. Cookies are very tender. Lift carefully with a spatula onto greased cookie sheet.

Cookies can also be cut with a donut cutter for the top half of the rounds. The mincemeat peeks temptingly through the hole in the top.

Bake 10 to 15 minutes at 350°F. Cool on racks, then hide them! Makes about 3 dozen cookies, depending on cutter size.

Norene Morris
is a gifted writer of inspirational romance.
Her titles include Rainbow Harvest
and Cottonwood Dreams
(Heartsong Presents).

CHOCOLATE PEANUT BUTTER COOKIES

½ cup sweet butter
½ cup sugar
½ cup brown sugar (lumps
    removed)
1 cup crunchy peanut butter
1 large egg

½ teaspoon vanilla
1¼ cups flour
¾ teaspoon baking soda
¼ teaspoon salt
1 small bag Hershey Kisses

Cream butter, peanut butter, sugars, egg, and vanilla. Sift dry ingredients. Blend into mixture. Shape into 1-inch balls; roll in granulated sugar. Place 2 inches apart on an ungreased cookie sheet. Make crisscross lines with fork tines. Place one Hershey Kiss on top of each cookie. Bake at 350°F for 10 to 12 minutes. Cool and remove from sheet.

Lindy Penevolpe
resides in
Bayville, New Jersey.

CANDY CANE COOKIES

This recipe is my personal favorite because of the decorative design it adds to a plate of cookies and also because I enjoy the taste of a soft brownie with peppermint icing.

Combine ⅜ cup hot water with 1 package dry devil's food cake mix. Mixture will be lumpy. If necessary, add drops of water very sparingly.

Roll into narrow logs about 8 inches long, curving one end to form the shape of a candy cane. Bake 8 to 10 minutes at 350°F on a greased cookie sheet.

When cooled, frost cookies in white: 3 cups sifted confectioner's sugar, 3 tablespoons hot water, 9 drops peppermint. Use red cake icing in a tube to add stripes.

Michelle C. Hooks
resides in
Apopka, Florida.

Twenty-five years ago a friend gave me her mother's recipe for fruit cookies and I have made them at Christmas ever since. Although a lot of children don't like fruitcake, they love these cookies.

7 cups pecans
1 pound candied cherries
1 pound candied pineapple
8 ounces dates
2 sticks margarine or butter
3 cups cake flour (plain)
1 teaspoon baking soda
1 teaspoon cinnamon
½ cup milk
1 cup brown sugar
3 eggs

Chop all fruit and nuts into small pieces. Mix fruit with 1 cup of the flour and add nuts. (You can do this in a paper bag.) Cream butter and sugar. Add beaten eggs and mix well. Add cinnamon and baking soda to the remaining two cups of flour. Add milk alternately with flour to batter. Add fruit and nuts to batter and mix well. Drop by spoonfuls on greased (or sprayed) cookie sheets. Bake 20 to 30 minutes at 350°F. Place on cake racks to cool. Makes 12 to 15 dozen and freezes well.

Mrs. Willie Paul
resides in
Lexington, Kentucky.

The Family Treasury of Great Holiday Ideas

For the past two decades, the Christmas cookie-baking season has found me measuring ingredients from a 100-year-old German recipe. Blending molasses, nuts, citron, cinnamon, and lemon and orange peel into several cups of flour produces not only an irresistible cookie, but also allows me to say "Thank you" again to the woman whose casual comments changed my life.

I was 12 the summer I met my elderly neighbor's niece Doris Schumacher, who taught English and social studies in Minneapolis. Since school teachers frightened me, I was immediately intimidated by her, too. But she smiled and chatted with me about the classes I'd take that fall. Then she commented that I was undoubtedly nervous about going into junior high, but that I'd do just fine.

No one had ever talked to me like that before. (I usually heard only "How's school?" from adults.) By the time I walked across the street and up our front steps, I was determined to be a teacher "Just Like Doris!" None of the women in my extended family had attended college, so my announcement was a bit unsettling to some of the relatives. But I tucked the dream into my heart and, with God's grace and my perseverance, gained the degree that gave me 15 years in a Detroit-area classroom. Later, that same degree opened the door for me to pursue an editing career and rebuild my life after my husband died.

Doris is 90 now, but we've kept in contact since my family purchased her aunt's home. Always she has continued to encourage me. One snowy morning, she commented about how far I've come since my school days.

"Well, you're a big part of that success," I said. "You gave me the vision to go to college." Then I began to tell her about that long-ago five-minute meeting.

She interrupted me. "No, dear. The first time I met you was when you came to visit Aunt Minnie at the hospital after she'd broken her hip."

But I insisted the initial meeting had taken place the summer before I'd gone to the 7th grade. I described how she stood by

(continued on next page)

the large round table in her aunt's front room. The morning sun was coming through the lace curtains and fell across her brown and gray sweater that so beautifully matched her hair just beginning to turn gray. . . .

She paused for a long moment, then said, "Oh, my dear, I don't remember that at all."

I chuckled. "That's okay, Doris. It only changed my life!"

Now each year, I haul out my largest bowls in early December and relive that meeting as I bake the traditional Schumacher cookie — from the recipe Doris's mother wrote out a century ago.

Doris used to insist she didn't want me laboring over a detailed recipe when my life is already so hectic, but I, in turn, would insist that my gift of time was a way to express my gratitude. When she realized she couldn't dissuade me from making the cookies, she smiled. "They do make Christmas for me. My grandmother would be pleased that the family cookie is still being made. . . ."

Once, she confessed her envy that my daughter would help me with the cookies. Her own mother had died of cancer when Doris was 4; they had never baked together. But usually she described evening scenes of cracking and shelling the hickory nuts that would be stored in glass jars until the Great Baking Day. Her accounts of the wood-burning stove in the old kitchen and the mounds of cookies cooling on the table when she arrived home from school became as real to me as my own memories. I was especially fascinated that the baked oblongs were stored in stone crocks for several months.

One March her brother dared to mutter that he longed for a soft store-bought cookie instead of the ones that were now so hard they had to be dunked in coffee before he could bite into them. Even as an adult, he never forgot the stern glance from the grandmother.

These days, I bake those same cookies in a modern electric oven and store them in tins. But even with today's conveniences, I never forget the women who used to spend days preparing this traditional treat.

Here's the recipe:

(continued on next page)

The Family Treasury of Great Holiday Ideas

(continued for previous page)

1 quart (32 ounces) molasses
1 pound (16 ounces) light
  brown sugar
1 cup solid shortening
4 eggs, beaten
1 pint (16 ounces) sour cream
1 cup sour milk
2 pounds dark raisins
1 pound citron
½ pound (8 ounces) orange
  peel
½ pound lemon peel
6 cups nuts (I don't shell

hickory nuts; I buy black
  walnut pieces)
6 level teaspoons baking
  soda (in our high altitude,
  I use only 4½ teaspoons)
3 teaspoons baking powder
  (again high altitude: 3¼
  teaspoons)
12 cups unbleached flour
2 teaspoons ground
  cinnamon
1 teaspoon ground cloves
¾ teaspoon salt

Dissolve the baking soda in the sour milk. Set aside.

Heat the molasses and brown sugar in a large kettle. (Do not allow to boil.) Add the shortening to warmed molasses and sugar. Stir to dissolve.

Add the sour milk and baking soda mixture. This will bubble up quite a bit. Then add the sour cream and beaten eggs.

Coat the raisins, citron, orange peel, and lemon peel with a bit of flour. Set aside momentarily.

Add the cinnamon, cloves, baking powder, and salt to the 12 cups of flour.

Add the 12 cups of flour, raisins, nuts, orange peel, and lemon peel to the batter. Stir with heavy spoon.

On a well-floured countertop, roll out the cookie dough and cut into small rectangles. Place on a lightly floured cookie sheet.

The original recipe says, "Bake until done." I've translated that to 8 to 10 minutes in a 350°F oven. Enjoy!

Are these cookies tedious to make? Of course. Are they worth it? You bet! Not only is it my expression of appreciation for Doris's early encouragement, but it's my connection to generations of women who always go to extra trouble at the holidays for their families.

Sandra P. Aldrich
and her college-age children live in Colorado
Springs where she is the senior editor of
Focus on the Family magazine.

RELISH

MARG'S PEANUT BUTTER COOKIES

1 cup butter
1 cup brown sugar (light)
1 cup granulated white sugar
3 eggs, well beaten

1 cup smooth peanut butter
1 teaspoon vanilla
1 teaspoon baking soda
2½ cups all-purpose flour

Cream together butter and sugars; add well-beaten eggs, peanut butter, and vanilla. Sift flour and baking soda; add to mixture slowly and mix well. Take a small piece of dough in hands, roll it into 1-inch balls, and put on greased cookie sheet and press lightly with fork tines. Place in a 375°F oven for about 10 minutes.

Margaret Layton Hunt
resides in
Charlotte, North Carolina.

MINUTE-MADE MACAROONS

One 1-pound package shredded coconut
One 15-ounce can sweetened condensed milk
2 teaspoons vanilla

Blend coconut into milk. Add vanilla and drop by teaspoon onto well-greased cookie sheet. Bake 10 minutes (or until crusted but not brown) at 350°F. Cool 2 minutes before lifting individually with spatula.

Taken from: THE JUNE MASTERS BACHER COUNTRY COOKBOOK
by June Masters Bacher. Copyright © 1988 by Harvest House Publishers,
Eugene, Oregon 97402. Used by permission.

GINGERBREAD BOYS

Recipe makes a lot of boys!

1 cup shortening	½ teaspoon salt
1 cup light brown sugar	1½ teaspoons baking soda
1 cup molasses	2 teaspoons ground ginger
2 tablespoons distilled white vinegar	1 teaspoon ground cloves
1 large egg	1 teaspoon cinnamon
5 cups flour	½ teaspoon nutmeg
	1 teaspoon vanilla

Cream shortening and brown sugar together. Beat in egg. Stir in molasses and vinegar. Sift dry ingredients together. Add ⅓ at a time to egg mixture, beating until smooth. (You may have to use your hands.)

Chill dough for at least 3 hours. Cut off piece of dough and refrigerate rest until ready for it. Toss on floured tea towel or pastry cloth. Roll to ⅛-inch thickness; cut with cookie cutters dipped first into flour before cutting.

Place cookies on lightly greased cookie sheet and bake in preheated 350°F oven for 8 to 10 minutes, until edges brown. Remove to racks to cool before frosting.

ICING PAINT

1½ cups sifted powdered sugar	Dash of salt
2 egg whites	1 teaspoon vanilla

Beat ingredients at high speed. Put in small bowls and add coloring to each. Cover bowl with damp cloth until ready for use. Apply with a brush.

Note: If not planning to frost cookies, sprinkle with sugar or decorative toppings. (I freeze half the dough for another "cookie" day.)

Marabel Morgan
is the author of The Total Woman *(Revell)*
and other best-sellers. She resides
in Miami, Florida.

Taken from: Marabel Morgan, *The Total Woman Cookbook,* Fleming H. Revell, a division of Baker Book House Company, Copyright © 1980.

R E L I S H

Christmas has a German flavor at the Schenk farm in Rupert, Idaho. In early December Vi Schenk mixes up a triple batch of Date Nut Pfeffernusen cookies. She puts the cookies into a crock and lets them "ripen" until Christmas. Although the cookies taste best after sitting a few weeks, they rarely last that long!

2½ cups all-purpose flour
⅔ cup honey
⅓ cup sugar
1 egg
3 tablespoons buttermilk or
   sour milk
1 tablespoon shortening
1¼ teaspoons baking soda
½ teaspoon anise seed,
   crushed

¼ teaspoon salt
¼ teaspoon ground allspice
¼ teaspoon ground cloves
¼ teaspoon ground cinnamon
½ cup finely chopped dates
½ cup chopped walnuts
1 recipe Powdered Sugar
   Icing (below)
1 cup sifted powdered sugar

In a large mixing bowl, beat about half of the flour, the honey, sugar, egg, buttermilk or sour milk, shortening, baking soda, anise, salt, allspice, cloves, and cinnamon with an electric mixer on medium to high speed until thoroughly combined. Beat or stir in remaining flour. Stir in dates and walnuts. Cover and refrigerate overnight.

With floured hands, shape dough into 1¼-inch balls. Place 2 inches apart on a greased baking sheet. Bake in a 350°F oven for 10 to 12 minutes or until lightly brown. Cool on wire rack.

Coat the top of each cookie with Powdered Sugar Icing.

Place the 1 cup sifted powdered sugar into a clean paper or plastic bag. Place 6 cookies at a time into the bag; gently shake the bag to coat the cookies with powdered sugar.

Store in a covered container along with an apple slice. These cookies are best made several weeks ahead in order to soften them and blend the flavors. Makes about 40 cookies.

Powdered Sugar Icing: Mix 1½ cups sifted powdered sugar, 5 teaspoons milk, and ¼ teaspoon lemon extract.

Alice Schenk
resides in Rupert, Idaho.

3 cups flour
1 teaspoon nutmeg
1 cup margarine
¾ cup sugar
1 egg
2 teaspoons vanilla
2 teaspoons rum flavoring

Sift together flour and nutmeg. In another bowl cream together margarine and sugar. Blend into creamed ingredients egg, vanilla, and rum flavoring. Gradually add dry ingredients and mix well.

On lightly floured surface shape pieces of dough into long rolls, ½-inch in diameter. Cut into 3-inch lengths. Place on ungreased baking sheet and bake at 350°F for 12 to 15 minutes or until a light golden brown. Cool. Spread frosting on tops and sides of cookies. Mark frosting with tines of fork down the length of each cookie to resemble bark. Sprinkle lightly with nutmeg.

Frosting:

3 tablespoons margarine
½ teaspoon vanilla
1 teaspoon rum flavoring
½ cup sifted confectioner's sugar
2 to 3 tablespoons milk

Cream margarine with vanilla and rum flavoring. Blend in confectioner's sugar, alternating with milk, beating well after each addition until of spreading consistency.

Sharon Cofran Skinner
resides in
Pembroke, New Hampshire.

R E L I S H

Creating Christmas cookies has been a tradition in the Civitts family. As grandchildren come and go, with flour on their faces and delicious dough in and out of their mouths, this special time has molded and shaped their lives, making us a stronger family. The following recipe only gets better as the years go by.

2 cups sugar
2 eggs
1 cup shortening
1 cup milk
1 teaspoon baking soda dissolved in 1 tablespoon of water

Mix the above ingredients and add:
3 teaspoons baking powder
Pinch of salt
Nutmeg or lemon

Add flour (about 2 sifters full) until thick and pour on floured table. Knead. Refrigerate.

While dough is still cold, use desired cookie cutters (some handed down for generations!) dipped in flour to prevent sticking. Bake at 350°F. Frost and decorate when cooled.

Frosting: Mix together the following:

4x powdered sugar (¾ bag)
2 tablespoons margarine
3 tablespoons shortening
3 egg whites
Vanilla (or any flavor)

Julie S. Long Civitts
resides in
Toccoa, Georgia.

The Family Treasury of Great Holiday Ideas

Cream thoroughly:
½ cup soft shortening (part margarine)
½ cup sugar
½ cup brown sugar, firmly packed
1 egg

Stir in:
¾ cup buttermilk*
1 teaspoon vanilla

Sift together and add:
2 cups + 2 tablespoons flour
½ teaspoon baking soda
½ teaspoon salt

Add:
½ cup semisweet chocolate morsels
½ cup milk chocolate morsels
½ cup white chocolate morsels
½ cup walnuts, if desired
½ teaspoon grated orange peel (optional)

Chill dough. Drop rounded teaspoonfuls about 2 inches apart on lightly greased baking sheet. Bake at 375°F until set, but not brown, about 8 minutes. Makes about four dozen 2-inch cookies.

*Or ¾ cup milk with ½ teaspoon lemon juice

Variations: Peanut butter morsels and/or any combination of chocolate morsels may be used.

(Turn page for another recipe submitted by Sally Laity.)

R E L I S H

Cream together well:
¾ cup margarine
⅔ cup sugar
½ teaspoon baking soda
Pinch salt

Add:
1 egg, beaten
1 teaspoon Oil of Anise* with 2 teaspoons boiled water
2 cups sifted flour

Chill overnight. Roll out to desired thickness and cut into holiday shapes. Brush cut cookies with beaten egg and add colored sprinkles. Bake on ungreased cookie sheet at 325°F for 10 minutes, or until lightly browned. Makes two to three dozen.

*Note: Oil of Anise may be obtained at pharmacy. Do not use plastic measuring spoon to measure.

Sally Laity
is much in demand as a writer of inspirational
romance. Her titles include
Dream Spinner *and* Reflections of the
Heart *(Heartsong Presents).*
She resides in
Bakersfield, California.

PHEFFER KUCHEN

This recipe has been used on my mother's side of the family for many years. Every Christmas season my grandmother and aunt make these very hard German cookies.

½ pound sugar
2 cups butter
½ gallon dark syrup

Mix quite stiff with flour, let stand 3 to 4 weeks. Then mix in 3 teaspoons baking powder. Add enough cinnamon and nutmeg to taste. Add 8 to 12 eggs. Mix all together and roll out ¼-inch thick. Put peanuts on top and bake at 375°F on ungreased pan until done (about 12 to 15 minutes). My aunt recommends buying unsalted peanuts in the shell to be shelled out. Dip the cookies in coffee or tea, or expect a trip to the dentist!

Marcee Ekstrum
resides in
Sioux Falls, South Dakota.

POTATO CHIP COOKIES

2 cups margarine
1 cup sugar
1 cup potato chips (crumbled and heaped)

1 cup walnuts, chopped
1 teaspoon vanilla
3 cups sifted flour

Cream together margarine and sugar. Add potato chips, nuts, and vanilla. Sift in flour and mix well. Drop by teaspoonfuls onto ungreased cookie sheet and bake at 350°F for 12 minutes (or until brown). Cookies should look rough and chips should remain crunchy.

Taken from: THE JUNE MASTERS BACHER COUNTRY COOKBOOK
by June Masters Bacher. Copyright © 1988 by Harvest House Publishers,
Eugene, Oregon 97402. Used by permission.

RELISH

CHOCOLATE WREATHS

6 cups corn flakes
One 10-ounce bag marshmallows
¼ cup margarine
8 ounces chocolate chips
Green decorative sugar sprinkles
Cinnamon red-hot candies

In a large saucepan melt margarine; add marshmallows until melted. Remove from heat and add chocolate chips. Stir until melted. Fold in corn flakes until all flakes are completely covered. On waxed paper work quickly and form wreaths with mixture. Sprinkle with green sugar and decorate with cinnamon candies. Let cool completely and store in a cool place.

CHURCH WINDOWS

1 bag miniature colored marshmallows
One 6-ounce bag chocolate chips
One 6-ounce bag butterscotch chips
1 stick butter or margarine
1 bag shredded coconut
½ cup raisins or chopped nuts (optional)

Melt chocolate chips and butterscotch chips together with butter or margarine. Cool slightly. Fold in marshmallows and raisins or nuts. Sprinkle coconut onto waxed paper. Spoon chocolate mixture into a line that measures 2 inches wide by 12 inches long. Sprinkle more coconut on top. Cover with waxed paper and roll into tube shape. Chill until chocolate hardens. Slice and serve. Makes 16 slices per 12-inch roll.

Betsy Whitney
resides in
Old Tappan, New Jersey.

ENGLISH TOFFEE BARS

1 cup margarine
1 cup sugar
1 egg, separated

2 cups flour
1 teaspoon cinnamon
1 cup chopped nuts (optional)

Cream margarine and sugar together and add egg yolk; mix thoroughly. Sift flour twice with cinnamon. Add flour mixture to margarine mixture and blend thoroughly. Spread evenly in a greased 9 x 13-inch pan. Beat egg white lightly and spread over top. Sprinkle chopped nuts and press them into dough. Bake at 275°F for 1 hour. Cut into small bars while hot and then cool and remove from pan.

CHOCOLATE CHIP BARS

½ cup butter
⅓ cup sugar
⅓ cup packed brown sugar
1 egg
1 cup flour

1 teaspoon vanilla
½ teaspoon baking soda
½ teaspoon salt
½ cup chocolate chips
½ cup nuts (optional)

Soften butter with sugar, add rest of ingredients, and mix well. Spread into greased 9 x 13-inch pan and bake at 375°F for 15 minutes or until golden brown. (Chocolate chips may be substituted for nuts.)

Linda Caughey
resides in
Ithaca, New York.

R E L I S H

53
R E L I S H

1 cup raisins
½ cup water
½ teaspoon baking soda
1 cup sugar
½ cup shortening (not margarine)
1 teaspoon vanilla
1 egg
2 cups flour
1 teaspoon baking powder
½ teaspoon salt
½ teaspoon cinnamon
1 cup candied red cherries
½ cup nuts

Cook raisins in ½ cup water for 5 minutes. Add ½ teaspoon soda and cool. Cream shortening with sugar. Add egg and vanilla and beat. Add raisins, nuts, and cherries (these cherries should be ground finely in a food processor). Sift dry ingredients and add to fruit mixture. Refrigerate the dough for 30 minutes. Roll into 1-inch balls and place on a greased cookie sheet. Bake 15 to 20 minutes at 350°F. Makes about 50 cookies. This is a chewy, pink cookie.

(See facing page for another recipe submitted by Irene B. Brand.)

1½ cups sugar
¼ cup orange juice
¼ teaspoon salt
Water
3 cups cranberries
1 cup seeded raisins
1 tablespoon cornstarch
1 teaspoon grated orange rind
2 tablespoons butter

Make pastry for two-crust 9-inch pie. Bring first 3 ingredients and 2 tablespoons water to boil in saucepan, stirring until sugar is dissolved. Add cranberries and cook, stirring occasionally until berries pop open. Add raisins. Blend cornstarch and 2 tablespoons water. Add to berry mixture and cook until thickened, stirring. Remove from heat and stir in fruit rind and butter. Pour into bottom crust. Add 2 tablespoons butter and cover with top crust. Bake 25 minutes at 425°F. Serve hot or cold. Good with whipped cream or a scoop of frozen vanilla yogurt.

Irene B. Brand
is a well-known writer
of inspirational romance.
Among her titles is
Heartstrings (*Heartsong Presents*).

PUMPKIN BANANA PIE

3 medium bananas, quartered
1 cup canned pumpkin
1 cup evaporated skim milk
3 eggs, beaten
¼ cup firmly packed brown sugar
1 tablespoon all-purpose flour
1 teaspoon ground cinnamon
½ teaspoon ground nutmeg

Place bananas in container of blender or food processor and blend until smooth. Add pumpkin, milk, eggs, sugar, flour, cinnamon, and nutmeg. Blend 30 seconds more or until smooth. Pour mixture into Gingersnap Crust. Bake at 350°F for 45 minutes or until a knife inserted in center comes out clean. Serve at room temperature or chilled.

GINGERSNAP CRUST

1 cup gingersnap crumbs
2 tablespoons melted margarine
Vegetable cooking spray

Combine crumbs and margarine in a small bowl. Stir well. Press mixture into a 9-inch pie plate coated with cooking spray. Yields one pie crust.

Charlene L. Cragg
resides in
Moreno Valley, California.

MRS. WARREN'S BLACKBERRY COBBLER
(an old-fashioned country dessert)

Mrs. Warren, a character from one of my books, is famous for her family dinners. She always expects that her satiated guests can find a little space for a final helping of her blackberry cobbler. Her grandmother taught her to make it and she would be pleased if you asked for her recipe.

Crust:

Mix any standard biscuit recipe and roll out dough gently to less than ½-inch thick. Mrs. Warren admits that commercial biscuit mix works very well, but she does not approve of such shortcuts.

Use a clean (of course), greased mixing bowl to line with the whole round of dough. If you make a hole in the dough, pinch it shut; it won't show. Mrs. Warren uses a brown crockery 6-quart bowl. It is too big, but she likes it. She says a 3- or 4-quart bowl is probably all right.

Filling:

Mix just less than one cup sugar
2 tablespoons, a little rounded, cornstarch
Dash salt
3 cups blackberries, fresh or canned

(*Note:* If you are out of blackberries just now, you can use raspberries, or even canned sliced peaches with some of the juice.)

Fill crust. Fold the top closed like a giant dumpling. Dot the top with butter and sprinkle with sugar and cinnamon. Bake at 350°F for about 45 minutes to an hour, or as long as it takes to lightly brown the crust. Maybe you should start watching after about 30 minutes.

Serve warm with a big spoon, with or without ice cream. Cobbler tastes good cold too, if it lasts that long.

(*Turn page for another recipe submitted by Janet Gortsema.*)

MY MOTHER'S SNOW ICE CREAM

What better way to celebrate the first real snowfall of the season than by making old-fashioned snow ice cream! This is not the ice cream we are accustomed to buying from the store, but it is fun all the same.

Mix:
2 cups milk
2 eggs
½ teaspoon salt

1½ cups sugar
3 teaspoons vanilla

Gently fold in clean, fresh snow until the mix is at saturation. You should have about 1 gallon.

If you're not sure you will like it, try making half the recipe.

Janet Gortsema
is an inspirational romance writer as well as a
high school English teacher.
Among her titles is Design for Love
(Heartsong Presents).

SCRIPTURE CAKE

1 cup Judges 5:25
2 cups Jeremiah 6:20
2 cups Isaiah 10:14
1 cup Genesis 24:17
3½ cups 1 Kings 4:22

2 teaspoons Exodus 32:20;
   1 Kings 10:10
Pinch of Leviticus 2:13
2 cups 1 Samuel 30:12
½ cup Numbers 17:8, chopped

Mix well. Pour into greased pan, 12 x 8 x 2 inches. Bake at 350°F 40 to 45 minutes. Serve warm with butter.

We like to "swirl" a lemon and ginger glaze over top of warm cake—powdered sugar, ground ginger, and lemon juice.

Meta Stone
resides in Coeur d´Alene, Idaho.

The Family Treasury of Great Holiday Ideas

My great-grandmother, grandmother, and mother all used this recipe and it has become a family holiday tradition, especially at Thanksgiving and Christmas. The new generations of nieces and nephews still ask for and love this easy dessert.

The original recipe came from a dear family friend, an English woman, who had once cooked for royalty. This was one of her favorites, and royalty's, too!

2 cups sugar
2 cups water
2 heaping tablespoons shortening (do not use oil)
2 large finely chopped apples
1 cup walnuts (optional)

Boil together 5 minutes; let cool to tepid.

Sift:
3 cups flour
1 heaping teaspoon baking soda
1 teaspoon each—salt, cloves, cinnamon, allspice

Mix thoroughly.
Bake 35 minutes in 9 x 13 lightly greased pan in 325°F oven. Ovens vary, it may take longer. Bake until a toothpick inserted in middle comes out clean and cake is a shiny, golden brown.

Serve warm with whipped cream or cold (keeps well in freezer). Glaze with any powdered sugar glaze while cake is still warm or frost with cream cheese frosting—but it's still best warm with whipped cream.

Colleen L. Reece
is one of the most popular writers of Christian romance. Her titles include Whispers in the Wilderness *and* Silence in the Sage *(Heartsong Presents).*

RELISH

2 sticks butter
2 cups sugar
4 cups flour
4 eggs
1½ cups buttermilk
1 teaspoon salt
1½ teaspoons baking soda
2 tablespoons grated orange rind
1 cup dates (or raisins), chopped fine
1 cup pecans or walnuts, chopped

Preheat oven to 325°F. Cream butter and sugar. Beat in 1 egg at a time. Add flour and salt alternately with 1 cup buttermilk.

Add soda to ½ cup buttermilk and add to mixture, then stir in dates, nuts, and orange rind. Bake in well-buttered 10-inch tube pan for 70 minutes or until cake tests done. If using small loaf pans, 7½ X 3½ X 2-inch, bake 45 minutes. Test for doneness.

Sauce:

1 to 2 cups sugar
2 cups fresh orange juice

Heat sugar and orange juice until sugar is completely dissolved. When cake is done, let stand for 10 minutes; then spoon sauce over hot cake until all is used. It takes a little while to soak in. Let cake sit in pan overnight. In morning, remove to covered cake container.

Marabel Morgan
is the author of The Total Woman (*Revell*)
and other best-sellers. She resides
in Miami, Florida.

Taken from: Marabel Morgan, *The Total Woman Cookbook*, Fleming H. Revell, a division of Baker Book House Company, Copyright © 1980.

The Family Treasury of Great Holiday Ideas

PISTACHIO CAKE

1 package white cake mix
2 packages instant pistachio pudding
5 eggs
½ cup vegetable oil
½ cup water
½ cup milk

Grease tube pan and flour. Mix all ingredients together and bake at 350°F for 45 minutes or until toothpick inserted in center comes out clean.

Frosting:

1 package instant pistachio pudding
1 medium-size low-calorie whipped topping
½ pint heavy cream

Whip cream until stiff peaks form. Fold in pudding mix and whipped topping. Frost cake and dot with maraschino cherries. This makes a good cake to celebrate Jesus' birthday!

JoAnn Otto
resides in
Cortland, New York.

OATMEAL CAKE

1½ cups boiling water
1 cup oatmeal (dry)

Let these two ingredients set while you mix the rest.

1 cup white sugar
1 cup brown sugar
½ cup oil
1½ cups flour

2 eggs
1 teaspoon cinnamon
1 teaspoon baking soda
½ teaspoon salt

Combine all ingredients and bake at 350°F for 30 minutes.

Topping:
Boil: 1 stick butter, 1 cup brown sugar, and ½ cup milk or cream. Boil 3 minutes. Remove from heat and add ½ cup coconut and ½ cup nuts. Put on cool cake. It's a family favorite!

Rebecca Robbins
resides in Denmark, New York.

VICKI'S CHEESECAKE

Beat until smooth:

2 softened 8-ounce packages
cream cheese
2 eggs

1 cup sugar
1 teaspoon vanilla

Mix for crust:
¾ package graham crackers,
crushed

¼ stick butter, melted
1 tablespoon sugar

Pat in cheesecake pan. Bake at 350°F for 8 minutes. Pour mixture into crust. Bake at 350°F for 40 minutes; cool.

Top with the following: one 8-ounce sour cream, 1 teaspoon sugar, and ½ teaspoon vanilla.

Ellen Caughey
resides in Harrington Park, New Jersey.

The Family Treasury of Great Holiday Ideas

Luscious Coconut Cake

1 butter cake mix (prepared and baked according to directions
  in two 8-inch layers)
1¾ cups sugar
Two 8-ounce cartons sour cream
Two 6-ounce packages frozen coconut, thawed
One 9-ounce carton frozen whipped topping

When cakes are completely cool, split both layers.
  Combine sugar, sour cream, and coconut, blending well and
chill. Reserve one cup sour cream mixture for frosting and
spread remainder between layers of cakes.
  Combine reserved sour cream with whipped topping, blend
until smooth. Spread on top and sides of cake. Seal for three days.

Muggie Richardson
resides in
Yazoo City, Mississippi.

Elegant Peach Delight

1 box yellow cake mix
1½ sticks margarine, softened
1 large can peaches, drained
1 pint sour cream
3 egg yolks
Cinnamon

Combine cake mix and margarine. Press in lightly greased 9 x
12-inch pan. Arrange peaches on top. Beat sour cream and egg
yolks together. Pour over peaches, spreading sides of pan.
Sprinkle with cinnamon. Bake at 350°F for 20 to 30 minutes.
Serve warm or cold.

Ellen Nelson
resides in
Cresskill, New Jersey.

R E L I S H

HOLIDAY ALMOND CAKES

3 cups flour
¾ teaspoon baking powder
½ teaspoon salt
¾ cup slivered or sliced almonds
¾ cup chopped red glacéed cherries
1⅔ cups sugar
¾ cup butter or margarine
5 large eggs
2 teaspoons almond extract
1 cup milk

Stir together flour, baking powder, and salt. In small bowl
combine almonds and cherries. Sprinkle 3 tablespoons of flour
mixture over almonds and cherries. Toss until well coated. In
large mixer bowl, at low speed, beat sugar, butter, eggs, and
almond extract. Increase speed to high and beat for 5 minutes
scraping bowl occasionally. Reduce speed to low and beat in
flour mixture alternately with milk, beginning and ending with
flour mixture. Fold in almonds and cherries until evenly distributed (batter may look curdled). Spoon mixture into loaf
pans. Bake 50 to 55 minutes at 350°F or until toothpick comes
out clean. Cool cakes 10 minutes before removing from pans.

*Patricia Vetense
resides in
Palmyra, Wisconsin.*

The first Christmas my husband and I celebrated with his parents I was introduced to the Danish tradition of the hidden nut in the read pudding. We have enjoyed it each year since then. Since I am ow the grandmother, everyone comes to our home: our children, randchildren, and my husband's 88-year-old sister who was born n Denmark.

This is how it works: I prepare the pudding, putting small amounts n dessert dishes. My husband and I hide a slivered almond in two ishes: one for the adults and one for the grandchildren, so an adult and grandchild each win a prize. Then we mix them up until we don't ven know which dishes the nuts are in.

After the blessing, the pudding is served first, in small portions. The person who finds the nut is to hide it in his or her mouth, and veryone has to guess who has it. When we guess the right one, that erson shows the nut as proof. Then my husband hands each a prize, sually a gift of money. Oh, how delightful it is to see the children's aces!

DANISH BREAD PUDDING

cups whole milk
large eggs
teaspoons vanilla
⅓ cups sugar
¼ teaspoon salt

Enough stale french bread to
make 1½ cups, crumbled
¼ cup raisins (optional)
Nutmeg

Butter an 8-inch square glass baking dish. Preheat oven to 325°F.

Beat milk, eggs, vanilla, sugar, and salt together for about 2 minutes. Add crumbled bread and raisins; mix well. Pour mixture into baking dish. Sprinkle with nutmeg.

Bake for about 45 minutes to an hour, or until a knife inserted in the center comes out clean. Makes 8 to 10 servings.

Vi Jensen
resides in Grand Prairie, Texas.

R E L I S H

Christmas at the Cook family farm in South Georgia begins on th
day after Thanksgiving. Soon the house is decorated with a fres
tree, holly, magnolia, and fragrant white narcissus from the yard
and, of course, poinsettias. The air is filled with the scent of ha
and turkey. Ambrosia, sweet potato pies full of cinnamon, cakes
pecans, peanuts, and chocolate-covered cherries are consumed b
the fireplace. Ambrosia, a traditional dessert of the Old South, i
served in all of my books.

12 large navel oranges
Freshly grated or ½ can coconut
¾ cup sugar

Working over a large bowl to save juice, peel oranges and cu
across sections to form bite-size pieces. Remove any tough
membranes. Stir in sugar (to taste) and coconut. Cover and
refrigerate for 4 hours until very juicy. (Dessert will keep in
refrigeration for a week. It ay be made 3 to 4 weeks in advance
and frozen.) Serve in compote dishes plain or garnished with
whipped cream and cherry. Good alone or with cake and cook
ies. One serving per orange used.

Jacquelyn Cook
is a veteran inspirational romance author
whose books bring alive the late 1800s in
Macon, Georgia. Among her titles are
Beyond the Searching River
and River of Fire *(Heartsong Presents).*

½ cup apple, chopped
½ cup suet, chopped
½ cup molasses
2 eggs, beaten together
½ cup milk
2 cups sifted flour
¼ cup figs, chopped
½ cup currants
¼ cup candied cherries, quartered
½ cup raisins
¼ cup citron, sliced
1 tablespoon orange peel, chopped
¼ cup almonds, chopped
2 teaspoons baking powder
½ teaspoon each salt, baking soda, cinnamon, and nutmeg

Combine apple, suet, molasses, eggs, and milk. Sift flour, measure, and mix ½ cup with dried fruit and nuts. Combine remaining flour with baking powder, salt, baking soda, cinnamon, and nutmeg. Add to apple mixture. Add floured fruits and nuts. Turn into decorative greased molds, filling ⅔ full. Cover and steam 3 hours. Cool. Wrap. Freeze until ready to use.

Serve cold with hot hard sauce, whipped cream, or flambé at the table. Use your favorite mixture for flambé or simply dip sugar cubes in lemon extract and light. In any case, surround with holly and sprigs of mistletoe.

Taken from: THE JUNE MASTERS BACHER COUNTRY COOKBOOK
by June Masters Bacher. Copyright © 1988 by Harvest House Publishers,
Eugene, Oregon 97402. Used by permission.

RELISH

Note: This is a Fourth of July dessert (originally Red, White, and Blue) but my family likes it at Christmastime . . . hence, Red, White, and Green. Red is for the blood of Jesus; White is for purity; Green represents new life in Him. Amen!

1 box red Jell-O
1 box green Jell-O
3 cups hot water
1 envelope plain gelatin (1 tablespoon loose = 1 envelope)
½ cup cold water
1 cup half and half
1 cup sugar
1 teaspoon vanilla
8-ounce package cream cheese
½ cup walnuts

Allow each layer to jell (approximately 2 hours) before next one is made.

First layer (red): Dissolve box of red Jell-O in 2 or 1¾ cups hot water. Pour into oblong or square dish. Allow to jell.

Middle layer (white): Dissolve plain gelatin in ½ cup cold water. Heat half and half and sugar without boiling. Add this to gelatin mixture. Add vanilla and cream cheese and whip with mixer until smooth. Add walnuts and pour over first red layer. Allow to jell.

Third layer (green): Dissolve box of green Jell-O in ¾ cup hot water. Pour over the other layers. Let jell.

Serve plain or with whipped cream.

Carol Kirkelie
resides in
Canterbury, Connecticut.

The Family Treasury of Great Holiday Ideas

FAVORITE FUDGE

4½ cups sugar
1 tall can evaporated milk
½ pound butter (no substitutes)
Two 12-ounce packages chocolate chips
One 16-ounce jar marshmallow creme
1 cup walnuts, chopped
1 teaspoon real vanilla

Put chocolate chips and marshmallow creme into a large mixing bowl. Cook sugar, milk, and butter over medium heat. Stir constantly for seven minutes. Lower heat when boiling begins. Pour over chocolate chips and marshmallow creme, then mix for five minutes. Add walnuts and vanilla. Pour into a greased 9 x 13-inch pan . Refrigerate to cool. Cut in small squares.

Sylvia Soulian
resides in Alsip, Illinois.

BLUE RIBBON CHRISTMAS CARAMELS

2½ cups brown sugar
1⅓ cups white corn syrup
1 cup butter
One 14-ounce can sweetened condensed milk

Heat above ingredients over medium high heat in heavy saucepan. When mixture resembles softball — 240°F on candy thermometer — remove from heat. Add 1 tablespoon vanilla. Allow to cook 5 to 10 minutes on low heat and then pour into well-buttered 9 x 13-inch baking dish. Cool at room temperature. When firm, cut into bite-size pieces and wrap in wax paper.

Valerie Roberts
resides in Edgemont, South Dakota.

R E L I S H

Our family traditionally indulges in this dessert after Christmas dinner.

3 pints good quality ice cream (in the cylindrical containers)
1 pint chocolate ice cream
½ cup sliced almonds
Cherries and mint leaves for decoration
Mocha fudge sauce (below)

Set a long platter in the freezer to chill for at least 30 minutes. Slide a knife around the insides of the ice cream, then ease the ice cream out onto the chilled platter. Push ends together to form a log and smooth the joints with a spatula.

Freeze until firm, at least 15 minutes.

Soften the chocolate ice cream until it is the consistency of thick frosting. Working quickly, spread chocolate ice cream over the frozen log on the platter. Freeze until firm.

Garnish log with almonds, mint leaves, and half cherries. Slice and top with fudge sauce to serve.

MOCHA FUDGE SAUCE

1½ cups semisweet chocolate chips
¾ cup whipping cream
3 tablespoons strong coffee

Stir chocolate chips and whipping cream together over low heat until just melted. Stir in coffee. Serve warm. (This may be made ahead and refrigerated for up to a week.)

*Sara Everett
resides in
Hesperia, California.*

CHOCOLATE SCOTCH FUDGE

Melt together on low heat:
One 12-ounce package chocolate chips
One 12-ounce package butterscotch chips
1 cup condensed milk (recipe below)

Add: ½ teaspoon vanilla
       1 cup chopped nuts

Pour into a buttered pan, 9 x 13 inches, or smaller. Refrigerate. When cold, cut in squares.

Condensed Milk:
1 cup + 2 tablespoons instant nonfat dry milk
½ cup warm water
¾ cup sugar

Pour water into bowl; add milk and sugar and mix until smooth. (Set in a pan of hot water, if necessary.) I use my blender to mix it.

Elizabeth Hunt
resides in Ithaca, Michigan.

EASY POTS DE CREME

¾ cup milk   1 egg
1 cup (6 ounces) semisweet   1 teaspoon vanilla
   chocolate bits   2 tablespoons sugar

Heat milk just to boiling point. Place all ingredients in blender and add hot milk. Blend 1 minute at low speed. Pour into six individual dishes. Chill well and serve with whipped cream.

Rose Cabot
resides in
Norwood, New Jersey.

RELISH

1 cup chopped nuts
1 cup coconut
¾ cup sweetened condensed
  milk

2 small packages Jell-O
  (strawberry or assorted
  flavors)

Mix all together. Form into balls, roll in dry Jell-O, and let harden in refrigerator.

JUDY'S MICROWAVE PEANUT BRITTLE

1 cup raw peanuts
½ cup white corn syrup
1 teaspoon butter
1 teaspoon baking soda
1 cup sugar
⅛ teaspoon salt
1 teaspoon Mexican vanilla

Stir together peanuts, sugar, syrup, and salt in 1½-quart casserole. Place in microwave oven and cook 7 minutes, stirring well after 4 minutes. Add butter and vanilla to syrup, blending well. Return to microwave and cook 2 more minutes. Add baking soda, and quickly stir until foamy. Pour mixture onto lightly greased cookie sheet and spread out thin. When completely cool, break and bag.

Note: If roasted, salted nuts are used, omit salt and add peanuts after first 4 minutes.

Judy Boen
resides in
Bakersfield, California.

BRENDA BANCROFT'S CHOCOLATE WALNUT FUDGE

(Large batch)
4 cups sugar
2 sticks margarine
1 cup water
1½ cups powdered milk
28 large marshmallows
1 large bag chocolate chips
2 cups walnuts

(Small batch)
1 cup sugar
½ stick margarine
¼ cup water
½ cup powdered milk
7 large marshmallows
¼ bag chips
½ cup walnuts

Put sugar, margarine, and water in large saucepan. Boil for five minutes, stirring steadily. Add powdered milk, marshmallows, chocolate chips. When melted, add nuts and pour into buttered 9 x 13-inch pan. This easy and inexpensive fudge — it does not require keeping condensed milk on hand—has another advantage. Adding the powdered milk after the sugar, margarine, and water have boiled prevents candy from scorching in the pan.

Brenda Bancroft
is a pen name of inspirational romance author
Susan Feldhake. Her titles include
A Love Meant to Be *and* Indy Girl
(Heartsong Presents).

**OLD-FASHIONED
THANKSGIVING DINNER**

Cranberry-Orange Relish
Old-Fashioned Roast Turkey
Brussels Sprouts with Garlic Cream Sauce
Four Vegetable Purée
Perfect Pumpkin Pie

CRANBERRY-ORANGE RELISH

¾ cup sugar
Grated orange peel of 1 orange
Fresh-squeezed juice of 1 orange (this may be the same
    orange)
¼ teaspoon ginger powder
One 12-ounce bag fresh or fresh/frozen cranberries
1 handful of chopped pecans, toasted

To toast the pecans, place them on a cookie sheet or piece of
aluminum foil and toast under the broiler or in the toaster oven
for approximately three minutes. Pecans should be lightly
browned but not black.

   Combine everything except the cranberries and pecans in a
medium saucepan and bring to a gentle boil over medium heat.
Stir frequently until the sugar dissolves. Add the cranberries
and cook until the berries begin to pop, stirring occasionally
(approximately five minutes). Stir in the toasted pecans. Pour
the Cranberry-Orange Relish into a pretty serving bowl, cover,
and refrigerate until you are ready to use.

Preheat the oven to 350°F.

One 11-13 pound fresh turkey
Salt and pepper
Two 6-ounce packages
   cornbread stuffing mix
2 sticks butter
1 large onion
4 stalks celery
One 8-ounce can sliced water
   chestnuts
1 cup chicken broth

1 tablespoon fresh parsley,
   snipped into small pieces
1 teaspoon tarragon
1 teaspoon basil
¾ cup pecan pieces
Reynolds Oven Cooking Bag
   for turkey
1 tablespoon flour
1 large onion
4 stalks celery
3 tablespoons flour

Remove the neck and giblets from the inside of the turkey. Rinse the inside and outside of the turkey with cold water. Using paper towels, pat the turkey dry. Set aside.

In a large pot or Dutch oven, melt the butter over medium heat. If the butter starts to brown, remove from the heat until the vegetables are added. Meanwhile, peel and chop the onion and slice the celery. Add the onion and celery to the melted butter. Drain the water from the water chestnuts and add them to the celery-onion mixture. Cook until the celery and onions are soft. Add the freshly snipped parsley, the tarragon, and the basil. Add the cornbread stuffing mix and pecans. Stir to blend. Add the chicken stock and stir to blend. Season to taste with salt and pepper.

Lightly stuff the body and neck cavities of the turkey with the stuffing. Do not overpack the stuffing. There will be some stuffing left over. Close up the openings with the loose turkey skin and toothpicks or skewers.

Put 1 tablespoon of flour inside the cooking bag. Close the bag and shake it to dust the inside of the bag with flour. Sprinkle the inside of the bag with salt and pepper. Peel and slice the onion. Slice the celery. Holding the bag on its side, place the onion and celery in the bottom of the bag. Place the turkey inside the bag, on top of the vegetables. Close the bag

(continued on next page)

(continued from previous page)

with the fastener that is provided with the bag. Make 6½-inch slits in the top of the bag. The part of the bag being fastened should be at the end of the turkey, not on the top like a sack of trash. Place the turkey and bag in a roasting pan and put in the preheated oven 2 to 2½ hours.

When the turkey is finished cooking, remove it from the oven. Cut the bag open and carefully lift the turkey to a serving platter. Save the pan drippings for the gravy.

To make the gravy, put 3 tablespoons of pan drippings into a medium saucepan over medium heat. Add 3 tablespoons of flour and stir to form a thick paste. Add the remaining pan drippings ¼ cup at a time and stir after each addition. Do not add the remaining pan juices until the first ¼ cup is well blended and the gravy has thickened. Once it has thickened, add the next ¼ cup and repeat the process until all the pan drippings are used. A few drops of Kitchen Bouquet may be used to deepen the color of the gravy.

BRUSSELS SPROUTS
WITH GARLIC CREAM SAUCE

12 brussels sprouts
½ teaspoon salt
2 tablespoons butter
2 medium cloves garlic, finely chopped
½ cup whipping cream
½ teaspoon salt
Freshly ground pepper

Clean brussels sprouts by trimming the ends and removing all the damaged and tough-looking leaves. The part you use should look like a perfect little baby cabbage.

Cook the brussel sprouts in a medium pot of boiling salted water for about 10 minutes or until they are just barely tender. Remove them from the heat and rinse under cold water to stop

(continued on next page)

(continued from previous page)
the cooking process. Drain the water.

In a large saucepan, melt the butter over medium-high heat. Add the garlic and cook until the garlic is softened. Do not brown. Add the cream, salt, and pepper and bring to a gentle boil. Continue boiling until the mixture thickens slightly. Add the brussels sprouts and stir them until they are fully coated with the cream mixture. Serve 2 brussels sprouts per person and top with remaining cream sauce.

Four Vegetable Purée

1 medium onion, peeled and cut into eighths
2 medium turnips, peeled and cut into eighths
2 medium rutabagas, peeled and cut into eighths
1 pound carrots, peeled and cut into 1-inch pieces
6 cloves garlic, peeled
½ stick butter
Salt
Freshly ground pepper
Freshly ground nutmeg

In a large food processor, purée the vegetables in batches until they are all smooth. Return puréed vegetables to the pot and heat until any excess liquid is absorbed. Season to taste with the salt and pepper. The Four Vegetable Purée should be about the consistency of mashed potatoes. Serve topped with a little freshly grated nutmeg.

PERFECT PUMPKIN PIE

Preheat oven to 400°F.

1 unbaked pie shell

Filling:

One 16-ounce can solid-pack
   pumpkin (not pumpkin pie
   mix)
1 cup brown sugar
2 eggs
2 tablespoons butter, melted
1 tablespoon flour
1 teaspoon ground ginger

1 teaspoon cinnamon
½ teaspoon freshly grated
   nutmeg
½ teaspoon salt
½ teaspoon freshly grated
   pepper
¾ cup milk
¾ cup whipping cream

Mix everything except the milk and cream in a large bowl and stir
until they are well blended. Add the milk and cream. Stir until the
entire mixture is well blended and has an even color. Pour the filling
into the pie shell. Bake in the preheated oven at 400°F for one hour
and ten minutes. When the pie is done, it will be evenly risen and the
center will be fairly firm when it is shaken. To serve, cut the pie into
six even wedges and top with Whipped Cream Topping.

WHIPPED CREAM TOPPING

1 cup whipping cream
1 teaspoon vanilla

1 tablespoon sugar

Using an electric beater, beat the whipping cream in a medium
bowl until it forms soft peaks. (It will make a slight mound
when the beaters are lifted out. Beater must be turned off before
you check this.) Add the vanilla and sugar and beat just until
they are blended.

Marita Littauer
is a popular Christian seminar leader, author,
and speaker. Her books include
HomeMade Memories *(from which this*
excerpt was taken) and Giving Back *(Harvest*
House Publishers).

The Family Treasury of Great Holiday Ideas

Breakfast Casserole
Biscuits Delight
Christmas Morning Coffee Cake
Jalapeño Cheese Grits

The following recipes can be made days or weeks in advance and refrigerated or frozen. Serve with fresh fruit, juice, and coffee or tea.

BREAKFAST CASSEROLE

6 to 8 slices white bread
Butter or margarine
1 pound sausage, cooked and drained
6 ounces shredded cheese (1½ cups)
6 eggs, beaten
2 cups milk
1 teaspoon salt

Remove crust from bread and butter on both sides. Place bread in bottom of 9 x 13-inch pan. Spoon sausage and cheese over bread. Mix together eggs, milk, and salt., Pour over sausage and cheese. Cover and chill, at least overnight, or freeze.

When ready to cook, bake at 350°F for 45 minutes.

RELISH

4 pans dinner rolls (2 dozen to a pan)
2 sticks margarine
3 tablespoons poppy seeds
3 tablespoons mustard
1 small onion
1 teaspoon Worcestershire sauce

Melt margarine and mix with other ingredients.

Then mix together 1 pound shredded ham (they will shred it when you buy it in the deli), and ⅓ pound grated Swiss cheese.

Cut rolls in half, cutting the entire tray at a time. Spread ham and cheese mixture on bottom half. Put top half on and spread the butter mixture on top. Heat in 350°F oven until cheese melts.

(To freeze, put rolls back in original bag and freeze. When ready to use heat at that time.)

CHRISTMAS MORNING COFFEE CAKE

Grease and flour two loaf pans. Sprinkle part of the sugar mix on bottom of each pan before putting batter in pans; put rest of sugar mix on top and swirl it into the cake mixture.

Sugar Mix:
½ cup sugar
2 teaspoons cinnamon
½ cup pecans

Batter:
1 box yellow cake mix
1 box instant vanilla pudding
¾ cup vegetable oil
¾ cup water
½ teaspoon vanilla
4 eggs
¼ teaspoon butter extract

Bake 50 to 60 minutes in 350°F oven. While the cake is warm, dribble over the top a mixture of 1 cup powdered sugar, 3 tablespoons milk, and ⅛ teaspoon butter extract. Cool entirely in pan.

The Family Treasury of Great Holiday Ideas

4½ cups water
1 teaspoon salt
1½ cups quick-cooking grits
4 cups (1 pound) shredded Cheddar cheese
¼ cup butter or margarine
2 jalapeño peppers, seeded and chopped
2 tablespoons pimiento (optional)
2 tablespoons salt
3 eggs, beaten

Combine water and 1 teaspoon salt in a large saucepan; bring to a boil. Gradually stir grits into water; cover, reduce heat to low, and cook 5 minutes, stirring occasionally. Add cheese and butter; stir until melted. Stir in peppers, pimiento, and 1 teaspoon salt.

Add a small amount of hot grits to eggs, stirring well; stir egg mixture into the remaining grits. Pour grits into a lightly greased 12 x 8 x 2-inch baking dish. Bake uncovered at 350°F for 30 minutes. Yields 8 to 10 servings.

Allyson Overstreet
resides in
Coral Springs, Florida.

RELISH

Cranberry Juice
Sausage Fondue
Curried Fruit or
Cut-up Fresh Fruit Bowl

Holiday stollen or coffee cakes

The sausage is especially nice to have during the holiday since it may be frozen ahead. In our home it is a favorite on Christmas morning and can be baking while gifts are being exchanged.

SAUSAGE FONDUE

8 slices bread, cubed
  (including crusts)
2 cups grated sharp cheese
1½ pounds link sausage
4 eggs

2½ cups milk
¾ teaspoon dried mustard
1 can mushroom soup
½ cup milk

Place bread in bottom of 8 x 12-inch greased casserole. Top with cheese. Brown sausage and drain. Place on top of cheese. Beat eggs with milk and mustard. Pour over bread mixture and refrigerate overnight. (The casserole may be frozen at this point.) The next day dilute mushroom soup with ½ cup milk, pour over top, and bake 1 to 2 hours at 300°F until set. (If you are on a low-fat diet, you may use turkey sausage and egg substitutes. Loose sausage may be used as well.)

CURRIED FRUIT

⅓ cup butter or margarine
¾ cup brown sugar
4 teaspoons curry
1 no. 2 can crushed pineapple
1 no. 303 can pears
6 maraschino cherries
1 no. 303 can peaches or apricots

Melt butter and add sugar and curry. Drain and dry fruit. Arrange fruit on bed of crushed pineapple in 1½-quart casserole and pour mixture over it. Bake 1 hour uncovered at 325°F. Recipe can be made ahead and refrigerated.

Hermine and Al Hartley
are the successful author - illustrator team
responsible for The Family Book of Manners
(Barbour Books).
Al Hartley has been the cartoonist of the Archie
Comic series for over twenty-five years.

My heart for very joy doth leap,
My lips no more can silence keep;
I, too, must sing with joyful tongue,
That sweetest ancient cradle song.

Martin Luther

REFLECT

*A Treasury
of Holiday Writings*

CONTENTS

Note: The following story is told by my mother, Pearl Towne Reece, who went on to celebrate eighty-one more Thanksgivings after this eventful one. Never did a Thanksgiving morning dawn that she didn't remember the unseen menace that stalked four children along a woodland trail; the silent prayer of a frightened child; and an old hermit in a cabin doorway, lifting his hand in blessing.

It was 1910, and I had just turned thirteen. Thanksgiving Day was sunny, crisp, and cold. Long before dawn, our household in the little logging town was stirring. For the very first time we were to have a whole pig, roasted with an apple in its mouth! The pantry shelves were laden with every kind of cake and pie imaginable. I could hardly wait for afternoon and our feast.

But before we celebrated our own day of thanks, we children had something special to do. An elderly friend, a hermit, lived about two miles from town on a little homestead carved into the forest. Today Mama packed goodies in big baskets, and I, along with my ten-year-old brother, Ed, and two of my sisters, Myrtle, fifteen, and Vi, six, started down the long road to "take Thanksgiving to Mr. Fraser."

The road was little more than an overgrown, seldom used trail. Tree branches interlaced overhead, giving us the feeling we were walking in a green tunnel.

We wondered at the birds and animals that peered at us from behind tree trunks or fallen logs as we strode along.

"Snow on the mountain tops," Myrtle explained. "It drives the animals down."

"I can hardly wait to get to Mr. Fraser's." Ed ran ahead a little way balancing his burden carefully. "Remember when he made split pea soup for us?"

"And when he gave us apples?" Vi put in, rosy cheeks shining in the cold air.

"We won't want anything to eat today," I said as I closed my eyes, thinking of the pig roasting and the loaded pantry shelves.

The two miles vanished beneath our eager feet, and we arrived in the little clearing where Mr. Fraser's cabin stood.

Originally published in *The Ruralite*, November 1981.

R E F L E C T

"Why children!" Surprise filled his greeting. "What have we here, and on Thanksgiving Day, too!"

"That's why we came." We set down our offerings, delighted at his happiness. "You wouldn't come to our Thanksgiving, so we brought Thanksgiving to you."

"Well, if this isn't nice! You know, I just don't go any-where"—his gaze embraced his cabin and clearing—"but I really appreciate all this good food."

"We can't stay, Mr. Fraser," Myrtle told him. "All our guests are coming, so we have to get back."

"God bless you, children. You've made a happy day for me." Our last sight of him was standing in the doorway of his cabin, with his hand raised in farewell.

"Maybe I'll be a hermit when I grow up," Ed kicked a stone in the path.

"Not you. You like company too much." I didn't wait for an answer, but walked faster. "Let's go home. I'm hungry."

"You can't be! It isn't that long since breakfast." Myrtle was always precise.

"I am. Let's go!"

Our feet retraced the trail automatically, anxious to get back to the fun. About halfway there, we stopped to rest. Vi had trouble keeping up with the rest of us.

"I'm rested!" She smiled and jumped up. Then, "What's that?"

A low rustle came from the bushes alongside the old wagon track.

I could feel my heart leap to my throat. "What if it's a . . . ?"

Ed's face was pale. "It's a cougar; that's what it is."

Cougar! Every story I'd ever heard came rushing to my mind.

It was a cougar that attacked Joe Bennett, our surveyor. It kept rushing at him from the edge of the trail, but he beat it off with his knapsack until he got home.

A cougar had clawed a little ten-year-old Indian boy who was getting water for his village.

One cougar had come right into the yard of another Indian family living deep in the woods, and started to maul a five year old. The boy's sister had grabbed a chunk of wood and beat it off until help came.

I knew from the looks on my brother's and sisters' faces they

The Family Treasury of Great Holiday Ideas

were thinking of the same stories.

"Let's run!" I was up and ready to go, but Myrtle's fingers sank into my arm.

"No! Don't you know anything? Cougars are cowardly. They only attack when you're alone or if they are starved. Mama says we always have to stay together."

"But cougars . . . ."

I was stopped by the look in Myrtle's eyes. "Do as I say!" She gathered Vi close, and ordered Ed and me to follow behind. "Now holler and make all the noise you can!"

After a few tries I found I *could* scream, and while I yelled, my brain spun. *Surely God wouldn't let a cougar get us, especially not on Thanksgiving! Was He watching us?* Another rustle in the bushes sent a wave of fear through me, and I held Ed's hand tightly. *If You're there, please take care of us,* I prayed.

The trail we had so happily trod earlier that morning now became a murky nightmare. The rustling and swaying of bushes alongside the trail never stopped. We strained our eyes, hoping to catch a glimpse of our menace and being afraid we would. But only the moving brush bore witness to our silent companion. We shrieked until we were hoarse. At last we covered the final stretch of woods and burst into the edge of the open space that was town.

"We're safe," Myrtle gasped. "The cougar won't come out in the open." Even as she spoke there was a final rustle, a pause, then another rustle farther away, as if a long, sleek something crept along the ground.

We raced to the house, tumbling over each other to tell our folks what had happened. "A cougar . . . a cougar!" was all we could get out between gasping for breath.

When we finally managed to tell our story, one of the cousins was skeptical.

"Probably was just some old dog!"

Dad shook his head. "A dog would have come out in the open. It was a cougar all right." His eyes looked funny. I thought for a minute he was going to cry. "If I'd thought there was any danger, I wouldn't have let you go."

Mama was more practical. "Why should we have thought here was any danger? The McCulloch children walk in from their place every school day, and they're right in the heart of

REFLECT

93

the woods." She pulled us children closer, stretching out her arms until we all fit inside. "I'm just thankful God took care of these children."

I managed to find my voice. "Mr. Fraser said 'God bless you' before we left."

"I don't see why a cougar would be so close to town," one of the uncles said.

"The snow in the mountains drove it down." Dad pointed out the window to the high peaks glistening in the sun. "No food up there. The deer would be lower down. The big cats follow. This one must have been pretty hungry to follow people, even children." He grinned, but it didn't conceal the thankfulness in his eyes. "No Thanksgiving dinner for that cat!"

"Reub!" Mama's stern look stopped him.

"I was only joking, Eva," he said quietly. He looked at the four of us, still scared and shivering. "Must be about time to go check that pig!"

The cougar was forgotten. In the excitement of food and frolic, memories of that long walk dimmed . . . until a few days later, when Ed tore into the house, his face pale. "They got it!"

"Who got what?" I was busy and couldn't see why Ed had to be so noisy.

"The cougar." He stopped to gulp. "A hunter just brought in our cougar!"

"H-how do you know it's *our* cougar?"

"Because it was killed by the trail we walked. Boy, you should have seen it! It was half-starved, and . . . ."

I didn't hear any more. I was too busy shaking.

Colleen L. Reece,
who resides in Auburn, Washington, is a free-
lance writer and part-time teacher of creative
writing. She wrote A Torch for Trinity,
Wildflower Harvest, *and* Desert Rose
(Heartsong Presents).

Give thanks to God, who planned so well that
When He created humanity, there was already food, drink,
The sun, giving days in which to work and play,
And nights in which to rest and be renewed.

Give thanks to God for being faithful in His promises
For giving us the faith to know that we can go to Him
And He will be with us throughout our lives,
Wherever we may go, whatever we become.

Give thanks to God for showing us His love,
So great that He could give His only Son
To save us from our sins—and by *His* life and teachings
Show us how to love God, those nearby, and everyone.

Give thanks to God for our lives lived on earth
To care for His creation, including one another,
But also to prepare for that life we will live
With Him eternally—if we accept God's Son.

Dorothy M. Harpster
resides in
Lewisburg, Pennsylvania.

Copyright © 1993 by Dorothy M. Harpster

Thanksgiving Morning

There wasn't much going on that Thanksgiving. The turkey
was in the electric roaster in the kitchen. My dad and my
brother were at home. I was bored watching the parade on
television and I went into the kitchen to watch my dad pare
potatoes.

I remember his fingers so very well. He was able to get the
skin off the potato without taking half the potato with it, a task

REFLECT

I thought I would never master. He was listening to the local news on the radio that always sat on the counter and never had the station changed. It was a quiet morning, not much to say, but I enjoyed watching him work.

We bought rolls that only needed to be heated and browned and I thought they looked good. I thought they were so much "classier" looking than the ones my mom used to make from scratch. Mom would be home from work soon so I was put to work setting the table. I made placecards even though the four of us would sit in the same chairs—I was always wanting the illusion of entertaining. As a supervisor, Mom could have taken the day off, but she preferred to spell women who needed to travel to see families. I can't remember the actual meal that Thanksgiving, only the morning of preparation.

So why do I hold that morning so dear? My family attended other celebrations, many of them more festive. We always had get-togethers and even now my family has dinner at my mother's house on Sundays. The "family" now consists of twenty-seven members and counting. Every Sunday is like a Thanksgiving feast.

The reason is simple: My father was there. My dad died when I was sixteen. The days after he died I feared I wouldn't be able to remember his face. I couldn't remember the vacations, the parties, the things he told me. I worried that the man who had been such an important part of my life would just vanish from my memory. Now, fourteen years later, when I think of Thanksgiving, I can still see his hands.

Linda J. Beck
resides in
Chicora, Pennsylvania.

Stranger at the Door

Note: More than sixty years have passed since the incident in this story occurred. Three generations have heard the story and speculated—was it an angel sent to comfort and minister when needed? N

Originally published in *Guide* magazine, January 1983.

The Family Treasury of Great Holiday Ideas

one can say. I only know that because of this story, my own life has been influenced and my faith strengthened. Bill, the eldest son in this story, was my father.

It was a bitter night. The snow that had pelted the countryside during the day now swirled about with every gust of wind. The porch of the old house was covered with a thick carpet of white, and ice stood high in the water bucket.

Inside, the youngest child lay sick. The doctor had come earlier in the day, fighting his way through the winter storm. "Just be sure the baby stays warm," he instructed. "The sickness should run its course in a few days." He measured medicine into a small bottle. "Give this if needed." Then he was gone, anxious to get back over the five miles of clogged roads before dark.

For a time, there was quiet as the baby slept. Mrs. Trevor prepared the evening meal while her husband and the older boys struggled to the barn and settled the animals for the night.

"Whew!" Dad exclaimed. "It's really a howler!" Red-faced from the cold, he and the boys burst into the house, bringing with them the pungent smell of animals and shaking snow on the spotless linoleum. They quickly cleaned up and gathered around the table for a hot supper made even more welcome by the chaos outside.

"We have a lot to be thankful for," Mr. Trevor said. "Let's return thanks to God."

All heads bowed. "We thank You, dear Father, for this, Your bounty. We thank You for Your presence, and for Your loving care. Bless us all. In Jesus' name and for His sake we pray. Amen."

"Amens" echoed around the table, and the family loaded their plates. Above their happy conversation a hoarse cry arose from the corner. Mrs. Trevor picked up the flushed baby, concern shadowing her pleasant face. "Why, this child is burning up!"

"Anything we can do?" Bill shoved back his chair and went around the table to his mother's side.

"I don't think so. I'll sponge her off." Her hands caressed the fussy baby.

"Shall I ride for the doctor?"

Bill's question startled everyone. On a night like this? Yet he

REFLECT

would go if needed—and get through if anyone could.

"No. The doctor left medicine. He couldn't do any more if h[e] were here."

"Ma's a good nurse," Father said. "The baby will be al[l] right."

Mr. Trevor's simple statement brought some reassuranc[e] Mrs. Trevor *was* a good nurse; with so many children, she ha[d] to be.

Silently the younger girls cleared the table, washed and drie[d] the dishes, and put them away. The fireplace roared, radiatin[g] heat into the big room. The boys sat in front of it, each with hi[s] own job. On a big farm there was always a dozen other things t[o] be done. There was little time for moments of doing nothing.

As the hands of the clock crept slowly around their course the storm increased. "What was that?" Bill raised his head an[d] stood staring at the door. "No one in his right mind would b[e] out on such a night!" He crossed to the heavy door, swung i[t] wide, letting in a blast of night air.

A stranger stood on the porch.

"Come in, come in, man!" Bill motioned the stranger inside hastily closing out the wind that had set the curtains dancing "What are you doing out on a night like this?"

A slight smile crossed the face of the stranger. "I wonder might I have something to eat?"

"Of course." A thought struck Bill. "Will your horse nee[d] caring for?" He was halfway across the room when th[e] stranger's voice stopped him. "I have no horse."

"You're on foot?" Mr. Trevor's look met Bill's. What manne[r] of man would be without a horse, he wondered, in the middl[e] of a near-blizzard?

Mrs. Trevor spoke up, still busy with the child. "Don't kee[p] the poor man standing in his wet coat, Lewis. Help him get it of[f] and give him something to eat."

The girls were already filling a plate with the remains o[f] supper. Cornbread, still a little warm. Beans. A glass of mil[k] and some sweet pickle relish.

"I'm sorry it isn't more," one of them told him. Her hones[t] eyes looked into his. "It's all we have."

"This will be fine." For a moment his eyes rested on he[r] tangled curls and sweet face. A moment later the baby cried and he turned toward the corner.

"The baby's sick," someone said. "But Ma's a good nurse."

The stranger stopped with his fork almost to his lips. "The baby will be fine tomorrow."

Mrs. Trevor looked up, caught by the assurance in his voice.

Not wanting to embarrass the stranger by watching him eat, Bill and the other boys continued what they were doing.

The stranger finished. "Thank you for the food." There was simplicity, even dignity in the way he spoke. He rose. "I'll be going now." Before they could do more than stare, the stranger was into his coat and out the door.

"Bill, stop him," Father commanded. "He can stay here overnight. No one should be out . . . ."

Bill ran to the door, flung it wide, and stepped to the porch, shivering at the contrast from the warm kitchen. "Come back and stay with us!" he shouted. There was no answer.

Bill called again, "Mister, we have room for you to stay!"

Only the howling wind replied.

Bill stepped back inside, a strange look on his face.

"What is it, son? Where is the stranger?"

Bill swallowed, seeming to have difficulty in speaking. "He's gone."

"Gone! He'll freeze! Go after him and bring him back."

"I can't." Blue eyes met blue eyes. "Come out here." He opened the door again. His father and the other boys followed his pointing finger. "Look!" Before them lay the porch, the steps, the front yard, now lighted by the kerosene lamp Bill held high.

The snow was unbroken. *There were no footprints crossing the white expanse.*

Heedless of the blowing wind and snow the family stood staring at the unblemished snow. "But he went out that door! We all saw him. Where did he go?"

The boys could only spread their hands helplessly. They searched, but the only footsteps they found were those they made in their search.

"Ma says come quick!" one of the girls called.

The family rushed inside. "Is the baby worse?" Lewis demanded.

"No," Mother answered quietly. "The fever has broken. She is

REFLECT

sleeping naturally."

"Praise the Lord!" the exclamation from Lewis's lips shone on the faces of the others.

Bill turned from the sleeping baby to the door. . . . "He said 'The baby will be fine tomorrow.' "

"But who was he and where did he go?"

Bill shook his head at the eager little sister. "I don't know. Pa?"

Mr. Trevor started to shake his own head, then stopped. He crossed to the hearth where the big Bible always lay. His work-worn hands opened the pages and turned to a marked passage. His voice was unsteady as he read, "Be not forgetful to entertain strangers: for thereby some have entertained angels unawares" (Hebrews 13:2).

Mrs. Trevor asked the question hovering on all their lips. "You . . . you think the stranger was an angel?"

Lewis Trevor closed the big Bible. "I don't know. He came. We fed him. He said the child would be fine. I do not know that it was an angel. I do know there is no man who does not leave tracks in the snow."

Colleen L. Reece,
from Auburn, Washington, is a freelance
writer and a teacher of creative writing
courses. She has written such inspirational
romance novels as Angel of the North *and*
Legacy of Silver *(Barbour Books).*

A CHRISTMAS TIME THANKSGIVING

Dear God,

As Christmas time is drawing near
My heart is forced to think
Of all the things You've done for us
And the peace and joy You bring.

(continued on next page)

The Family Treasury of Great Holiday Ideas

(continued from previous page)

So God, please hear my prayer of thanks
As I share my heart with You,
My thoughts of love and gratitude
May Christmas time renew.

Thank You for, this child, Your Son
Who was born on Christmas Day,
Thank You for the joy He brings
In each and every way.

Thank You for His kind of love
That hung Him on the tree,
Thank You that He cared enough
For all the world and me.

Thank You for salvation
That He so freely gives,
Thank You that He rose again
Now, thanks to You, He lives.

Thank You for eternal life
That we can all receive,
The life that leads us home to You
If we will just believe.

Yes, thank You for this Christmas child
So precious and so dear,
Thank You God, for all You've given
To us this time of year.

Glenna Fox
resides in
Coeur d'Alene, Idaho.

R E F L E C T

In her book, *Secrets of Staying in Love* (Nelson, 1984), Ruth Peale, wife of Norman Vincent Peale, shares an intimate account with which many Christian couples can identify:

> When we were first married, we always had to go to Mother Peale's home for Christmas. "I may not be here next year," she would say plaintively if I suggested going to my parents or making other plans. So we always wound up going there . . . and I always had to control and mask my resentment.

Sound familiar? Don't feel bad—almost everybody has relatives who "probably won't be here next year, so we'd better spend this last holiday with them." Amazing, isn't it, the longevity of some of those dear ones?

Understand, we need to be sensitive to the needs of our soon-to-be-gone loved ones, whether gone means death or merely moving to a far-off or less accessible location. But it is unfair to stick your spouse's head (or yours!) in a guillotine of guilt. Don't do it, and don't allow other people to do it to you.

So how does one resolve those sticky holiday situations, especially Thanksgiving and Christmas? Some couples try to keep everybody happy by putting in an appearance at both parents' meal tables. Before I was married, I watched with amused interest as my brothers attempted that bulging balancing act.

For several years in succession, my brothers and their wives ate Thanksgiving or Christmas dinner with our family, then drove to the homes of their wives' parents and pretended they were famished in the face of another feast.

"Mmm-mm. Turkey and stuffing! My favorite. Haven't had a meal like this in . . . at least fifteen minutes!" Holidays meant one thing for my brothers and their wives: Pepto-Bismol.

After a few years of this gluttonous gobbling, my mother and dad proposed a compromise. "Let's have Thanksgiving or Christmas breakfast here, then you guys can go to your in-laws later in the day for dinner." It made sense—unless you happen to know my mother.

Excerpted from: Ken Abraham, *Unmasking the Myth of Marriage*. Fleming H. Revell, a division of Baker Book House Co., 1990.

The Family Treasury of Great Holiday Ideas

When my mom cooks a holiday breakfast, you could feed the entire Fourth Infantry. I've seen big-time hotel buffets that don't have a breakfast spread like my mother's. She gives you the works: ham and eggs, pancakes, sausage, bacon, cereal, juices, toast, cinnamon rolls, and waffles. If you can imagine it for breakfast, she'll prepare it.

Still, my brothers and their wives were a bit happier; at least they got a break between "pigging out" for breakfast and stuffing themselves at dinner. Both brothers began to resemble the Goodyear Blimp, but the in-laws were happy.

For several years, I watched this spectacle of holiday table hopping with bemused objectivity and pity. Then Angela and I got married. Now it is no longer mere table hopping—we engage in serious state hopping. We have Christmas breakfast in Pennsylvania with my family and Christmas dinner in Michigan with Angela's family. We feel fortunate, though. We have an entire turnpike between our breakfast and dinner tables.

We have also tried a variety of combinations in our attempts to be fair to both families. We've spent holidays at home and invited everyone to our home. We've spent Thanksgiving with one family and Christmas with the other.

What's the solution to such holiday hassles? Equality. Angela and I are travel addicts. We don't really mind driving five hundred miles in a day in order to spend the holiday with both of our families. For most people, however, equality will mean Thanksgiving with one set of parents, Christmas with the other; or perhaps alternating years, visiting one family one year and the other family the following year.

Whatever you do, don't allow those blessed, special times of the year to be destroyed by disagreements over where you will spend the holiday. Two principles are important in this regard: Consider creative alternatives and seek to compromise. Rather than fighting over family functions, look for alternative means of satisfying both sets of in-laws. Perhaps you might ask both of your families to get together at your place, or ask one family to invite the other, so you can celebrate together. Compromise is the key. Stay flexible and seek harmony and unity among your family members.

Ken Abraham
is the author of sixteen books. He lives in
Antioch, Tennessee, with his
wife and two daughters.

REFLECT

Christmas will soon be here.
a season we hold very dear.
A time to start to bake,
many good foods from which to partake.
For many gifts we begin to look,
a shirt, a toy, maybe a good book.
Another year, a beautiful tree,
many gifts under it, what could they be?
Secrets, mysteries, whispers, and bows,
music, candles, wreaths, and snow.

Wait a minute, slow down,
take time, let yourself be found.
Don't be in a constant hurry,
no need to run and scurry.
Relax, enjoy the holiday
for sooner than you know it will go away.
Savor every minute of this time,
for a memory it will soon be.

Joyce Friesner
resides in
Ligonier, Indiana.

All my heart this night rejoices,
As I hear, far and near,
Sweetest angel voices;
"Christ is born," their choirs are singing,
Till the air, everywhere,
Now with joy is ringing.

Paul Gerhardt

The Family Treasury of Great Holiday Ideas

The people's great concern was the census for Rome
and for that census they journeyed from home.
They crowded the streets and filled the inns
in that little town of Bethlehem.
The decree had been issued and must be obeyed,
everything else had to be stayed.
So that Caesar could know who belonged to him
and gather taxes from each of them.
On the holiest night the world has known
man's greatest concern was to be counted
for Rome.

But, in times long past, God's own decree
declared this holy night should be.
His gift would come to Bethlehem and
make amends for all man's sins.
On that holiest of all, the most blessed night,
Bethlehem glowed with heavenly light.
As the angels came and sang songs of glory,
shepherds were told the wondrous story.
And wise men saw a bright new star
and followed its light,
traveling far.
They kept the secret under careful guard
as they searched for the gift of
eternal reward.

But, men nearby failed to see
the miracle of God's decree.
Their eyes didn't notice the Bethlehem light,
that special star God gave that night . . .
Their ears were filled with the clamor in town,
and they couldn't hear the angels' sounds.
Caught in the midst of Caesar's plans,
people missed the beauty of that night—
God's gift to man.

R E F L E C T

Now, long years after, God's gift remains
to take away all our stains.
The gift eternal was God's decree—
Christmas in the world to set men free.
Wise men still seek the godly might
that came to earth that holy night.
Christmas was decreed from above
to bring into the world
God's peace and love.
Now, people on earth can one day be
citizens of heaven by God's decree.
Where census and taxes won't burden man
because giving to us is what God has planned.

Christmas everyday
for everyone . . .
God has decreed it through Jesus, His Son.

Annette Owens Selcer
resides in
Cincinnati, Ohio.

But while he thought on these things, behold, the angel of the
Lord appeared unto him in a dream, saying, Joseph, thou son of
David, fear not to take unto thee Mary thy wife: for that which
is conceived in her is of the Holy Ghost. And she shall bring
forth a son, and thou shalt call his name JESUS: for he shall save
his people from their sins. Now all this was done that it might
be fulfilled which was spoken of the Lord by the prophet,
saying, Behold, a virgin shall be with child, and shall bring
forth a son, and they shall call his name Emmanuel, which
being interpreted is, God with us.

(Matthew 1:20-23, KJV)

The Family Treasury of Great Holiday Ideas

Christmas is love . . . a time to celebrate God's gift of His Son, Jesus, and to build family bonds and blessings. We try to send a Christmas letter every year, updating family and friends on the happenings of our lives. Within this letter, we also share how God has touched our lives with His love and forgiveness. One year we used the following poem I had written to convey the beautiful message of the Christmas season.

> Bless our friends and family, too,
>   'tis the season for no more blues.
> Love came down and became a man,
>   so all will have the Salvation plan.
> Jesus is the Way, the Truth, and Life,
>   He conquered death and conquered strife,
> Left His Spirit to kindle our flame,
>   yielding temples as we proclaim
> No shred of hope apart from Him,
>   free of guilt and free of sin;
> Soon to give our spirit wing,
>   to fly away with our Savior and King.
> This message of comfort and peace, you see,
>   is truly Love's unending legacy.

*Julie S. Long Civitts
resides in
Toccoa, Georgia.*

I have made a covenant with my chosen, I have sworn unto David my servant, Thy seed will I establish for ever, and build up thy throne to all generations.

(Psalm 89:3-4, KJV)

REFLECT

We
sell
family
traditions,
we sell
fun and happiness,
we sell
cut-your-own Christmas trees
!!!!!!

We bought the rundown old farm when our children were little and my husband immediately began planting trees. As portions of the overgrown orchard were cleared, Bob set out apples, cherries, apricots, nectarines, plums, and pears. In one of the two tilled fields, we planted rows of evergreens, expecting these spindly plants to grow with God's sun and rain—and with little care from us.

But weeds, brush, and grass grow faster than trees, so we mowed and cut throughout the growing seasons. As the blue spruce and Douglas firs got larger, there was trimming and shaping to be done every year. And each year there seemed to be additional problems, from hunters trampling the seedlings to gypsy moths and sawflies that had to be destroyed.

Seven years postplanting, some of the first were big enough for Christmas trees. People came, wandered through the rows, and found just the right tree for them.

They and others returned the next year and those following. Families arrived with teens and toddlers, often spending joyful hours as each took part in the decision-making. As years passed and some trees got quite large, church and other groups made outings of their searches, while restaurants and banks also used our Christmas trees.

By keeping our prices very low (still $15 for *any* tree), struggling young couples, families, and even elderly singles could make room for one in their much-stretched Christmas budgets. Memories of good times in God's out-of-doors bring people

The Family Treasury of Great Holiday Ideas

back. We enjoy our visits with the parents who, once carried here as babies, now bring their offspring to roam the hillside and shout with joy at finding their tree.

We are blessed to be a part of many family Christmases!

Eileen M. Berger,
who resides in Hughesville, Pennsylvania, is
an award-winning author. She has written
several inspirational romance novels, two of
which are A Place to Call Home *and*
Escort Homeward (*Heartsong Presents*).

CHRISTMAS LISTS

December days are filled with lists—
the presents I must buy,
ingredients for cookies,
new recipes to try,
packages to mail, and
Christmas cards to write—
my lists defy completion,
though I labor day and night.
And as the month keeps rushing by,
the stress mounts and I find
a certain lack of purpose
in my ritualistic grind.
I need to put my lists aside
and seek what wise men found—
that "peace on earth" that angels sang
to shepherds all around.
For God's gift still comes quietly,
and as my heart is stilled,
my Christmas list becomes
a list of promises fulfilled.

Kathy Schriefer
resides in
Erie, Pennsylvania.

REFLECT

'Twas the night before Christmas and all through the town
    everybody was busy, it was time to "bed down."
The stockings were pulled on all feet to keep warm,
    a chill in the air caused a bit of alarm.

As little ones slept, others searched, some in vain
    for a warm place to sleep and keep out of the rain.
Mama in her kerchief, Papa in his cap
    had just gone to bed when they heard someone rap.

And out on the lawn was a sight to be seen!
    A man and his wife not looking too lean!
The donkey she sat on looked tired and spent,
    and they looked like they wouldn't have money for rent.

It looked like the woman would soon have a child,
    and the weather was really not what you'd call mild!
Papa felt a pang in his heart for these two,
    but his inn full of beds was filled up—what to do!

Mama to the rescue! suggesting the barn.
    'Twas better than nothing, and certainly warm.
So off they all went to see what they could do
    fresh hay in the manger—the baby was due!

With gratitude man and wife thanked the old pair,
    who went back to the inn, thankful they could share.
But later that night something woke them from sleep!
    A bright light lit the room, from their bed they did leap!

They looked out the window, and there not too far,
    was the biggest, the best, the brightest new star!
And over the hilltops some shepherds ran down
    and seemed to be searching through Bethlehemtown.

The Family Treasury of Great Holiday Ideas

Papa and Mama ran into the street
  to ask a good shepherd to rest his sore feet
And tell them what happened that caused such a stir!
  So the shepherd reported all that did occur.

He told of the angels who lit up the sky
  with God's glory—and told of a baby nearby
Wrapped in swaddling clothes, laid in a manger with hay
  in somebody's barn—and it's over this way!

It might be OUR barn they told the shepherd
  but what is so special about what you heard?
The shepherd reported to them what was said—
  The Savior! The Lord's in that small manger-bed!

The three on the run entered into the barn,
  and there on the hay the new baby kept warm.
The Savior it was! Of that they were sure!
  and "Jesus" they called Him—so perfect, so pure!

And in the short distance they heard angels sing
  "Glory to God, peace on earth, He's your King!"
What a wondrous event did take place that great night
  when Jesus our Lord came to do what was right.

To set an example, to show us the way
  to our Father in heaven who loves us always,
To pay for our sins which, ourselves, we can't do,
  by dying and shedding His blood for me and you.

The shepherds returned to the sheep on the hill
  with a song in the air of praise and goodwill.
Others came, rich and poor, in the days that went by,
  The star showed them the way, shining bright in the sky.

And today we remember the babe in the hay—
  MERRY CHRISTMAS TO ALL—FOLLOW HIM! HE'S THE WAY!

Jan Carlson
of Clayville, New York, was given this poem
from the Lord December 1991.

REFLECT

Rejoice! God's Son
in humble dignity
did come to save us
from iniquity.
Rejoice! His birth
is only but a part
of all that is
within God's heart.
Rejoice! God's gift
is ours to claim . . .
so we will be His
when Christ
shall come again!

Isabelle Giltinan Smith
resides in
Jamestown, New York.

Copyright © 1992 by Isabelle Giltinan Smith.
Appeared in December 1992 issue of DECISION magazine.

GOD'S CHRISTMAS TREE

When you put up your tree so pretty and bright,
Think of God's—Oh, what a sight.
His is the one at Calvary,
There He died for you and me.
His gifts are there—Oh, not a toy,
But rather forgiveness, hope, and joy.
His gift certificate from heaven above,
Come, receive, be filled with His love.
Hear Him calling to you and to me,
Oh, please come to His Christmas tree.

Kathy Offord
resides in Barron, Wisconsin.

The Family Treasury of Great Holiday Ideas

Christmas is coming and I, like most people, find myself getting excited. The sound of Christmas music, brightly decorated Christmas trees, giving and receiving of gifts, and time spent with family and friends all help to add to the excitement I feel about this special day.

But wait. Isn't there a much deeper meaning of Christmas? Of course there is for this is the day God chose to come to earth to live with us through His only begotten Son, the baby Jesus. Christmas is the birthday of Jesus Christ, our Savior and Redeemer, who lived with us, died for us, and saves us from our sin. What a wonderful and exciting Christmas gift God has given us because He loved us.

Oh yes. Christmas is exciting, Lord. It is my prayer that I never lose sight of this, Your day, and its deeper meaning.

Glenna Fox
resides in
Coeur d'Alene, Idaho.

CHAINS OF LOVE

Our daughter, Vicki, has always loved Christmas. Even when tiny, she delighted in helping trim trees, bake special cookies, decorate cakes, and invite others not only to enjoy but to participate in our activities.

Her first son was twenty months old when the second arrived six days before Christmas. Their tall Douglas fir was adorned with many items holding special memories and meanings, including bubble-lights that had brightened trees of Conrad's youth and dated balls commemorating Vicki's birth and other life events.

These treasures of their past were tied into their present with construction-paper chains. Near the bottom was one over six-feet

REFLECT

long, mostly in primary colors, above which was draped a five-foot nine-inch one of carefully selected hues. The next, less than a yard in length, had links not evenly pasted nor as "artistic," while the top one, in shades of blue, was twenty-one inches long.

The first three family members had made their own, to their exact heights, and even Isaac's infant fingers had been pressed against some of his links as circles were joined together into chains. Two years later, baby Samuel's festoon joined his brother's, which by then had been made longer.

Struggles and difficulties have taken place in their lives the four years since then, but joys and togetherness continue to triumph. The paper chains are delicate and carefully put away between Christmases, but their family experiences and memories make their *life*-chains ever-present, ever-stronger, created as they are with love, encouragement, faith, and doing things together.

Eileen M. Berger,
author of many fine inspirational novels,
wrote Lexi's Nature *and* Tori's Masquerade
(Barbour Books).

A SPECIAL CHRISTMAS TREE

The tree was standing in the corner of the room, its branches still bare, and boxes of Christmas decorations were sitting on the floor. I really wasn't in the mood for decorating the tree that day, yet I wanted it ready for when the children and grandchildren came for Christmas.

I also wanted that tree to look extra beautiful that year and, while thinking about some new way to make the tree look special, I suddenly got a great idea—why not decorate the tree with the large, inexpensive, colored cut-glass pins that I had been collecting all these years! They were out of style and had no real use but I liked the way the light shone through the colored glass. I put a little wire hook on each one and hung them from the branches of the tree. When all of them were on, I stood back to look. Light from the window shone through each jeweled pin, making a rainbow of many colors on the tree. It was as if hundreds of tiny colored diamonds were hanging on the branches—it was a tree that would be remembered.

Our house is small and when all of the children come home with their families it is crowded. My daughter-in-law spotted the jeweled Christmas tree in the corner and said, "Look, we have the only tree in the world that is decorated with jewels!" Everyone agreed that the sparkling tree was special.

I had covered mats and pillows with Christmas material and the children were excited when we told them they could sleep on them by the tree. That night they didn't complain about going to bed. With the tree lights on, each jeweled decoration sparkled and, as the children heard their Bible story before going to sleep, the lights shone down on their happy faces. They would never forget the night they slept by Grandma and Grandpa's jeweled tree and they would someday tell their children about the Christmas tree covered with jewels, fit for a King, whose birthday they had celebrated at their grandparents' home.

Gloria Zeisler
resides in
Santa Ana, California.

REFLECT

Martha's Christmas trimmings
    were a decorator's dream—
Her tree a dazzling masterpiece
    that fit the color scheme.
The gifts, all wrapped creatively,
    lent just the perfect touch.
The windows shone; she wondered if
    the snow would streak them much.
When Jesus came, she quickly brought Him
    all her best hors d'oeuvres
Then bustled to the kitchen,
    for she had a meal to serve.

When Jesus came to Mary's house.
    the tree was small and plain,
Trimmed with childish ornaments
    and homemade paper chains.
But Mary smiled warmly,
    and said, "I'm glad you came!"
They popped some corn, drank lemonade,
    and laughed while playing games.
They talked and shared for hours,
    and when the night was through,
Mary begged Him, "Come back soon—
    there's always room for You!"

Kathy Schriefer
resides in
Erie, Pennsylvania.

My mother was visiting us during the Christmas season. One day, on a walk, she stopped at a little store that was having a sale. Among her bargains most of all I liked some little plastic choirboy decorations. I went back to the store and got all the choirboys that were left. They were selling for only ten cents each.

When we got our tree I had fun putting on all the choirboy decorations. As a finishing touch, I added a plastic angel to the top of the tree. The angel, a favorite decoration, had been on our Christmas tree year after year. As I stood back to inspect at the tree, it just looked perfect! I had a record of choirboys singing and imagined we could play that on Christmas Day.

Later that evening when it was time for bed I pressed the switch to turn off the light. I discovered then that I had got more for my money than I had known. I had received a Christmas surprise. Every choirboy decoration hanging on the tree was glowing in the dark—the whole tree was aglow with light!

The decorations have since been used many times. Each time I take them from the box, memories of past Christmases flood my mind. Each of the grandchildren likes to hold a little choirboy in his hand at bedtime to watch it glow in the dark. Some of the little decorations were given to them to take home and put on their tree.

I will never forget that night long ago when the choirboy decorations shone so bright for the first time. I felt like singing. I knew that Jesus, The Light of the World, had come to bring joy. I knew that He had sent this Christmas surprise to me, just to make me happy.

Gloria Zeisler
resides in
Santa Ana, California.

REFLECT

It was the week before Christmas 1983 and I was feeling very alone. It would be the first Christmas for the children and me since Don's death. I had tried hysteria that December day and found that tears wouldn't ease my grief. Convinced that my sanity would be retained only if I could look beyond my widowhood and help someone else, I called the local Salvation Army and volunteered us for whatever needed doing.

I had no problem getting eleven-year-old Jay and nine-and-a-half-year-old Holly to agree to go. They'd grown up doing unusual things with me, their goofy mother. Besides, we'd already spent Thanksgiving helping feed street people.

As I pulled my new gray coat from the front closet, I glanced at my older one still on the hanger. Had I been too extravagant in getting this one? Should anyone have two gray coats?

I shut the door and quickly buttoned my collar. Didn't I have enough to worry about without adding guilt to the list?

When we pulled into the parking lot behind the Salvation Army headquarters, several people were waiting for the building to open. How cold they looked as they stood with their heads down, their backs to the bitter wind.

When we entered through the back door, volunteers were already sorting canned goods and toys. They needed someone to deliver the holiday food. We accepted the assignment.

The first delivery was up a set of rickety steps to an apartment over a downtown store. An elderly woman opened the door cautiously, waiting for me to identify myself. Her eyes settled immediately upon the red Salvation Army badge pinned to my coat collar. Then she grinned as she saw Jay and Holly smiling up at her.

She started to speak but instead cleared her throat several times, as though she wasn't used to talking. Finally, she gestured to the table sitting in the middle of the one room that served as living room, bedroom, and kitchen. I unpacked the small turkey, potatoes, canned green beans, cranberry sauce, and rolls.

The Family Treasury of Great Holiday Ideas

"Is all this for me? Are you sure they haven't made a mistake? Why, that's a feast!" Her eyes sparkled.

I wondered how long it had been since the stark room had heard so many words.

"Oh, I know there's no mistake," I said. "The social services director at the Salvation Army gave me your name himself."

Her aged face crinkled into a grin.

We said our goodbyes and I went out the door a little happier than when I had climbed those dark stairs.

The next stops were to more one-room apartments and tired houses. We three carried in the bags, stayed momentarily to hear about grandchildren who looked like Jay and Holly, and heard excuses why adult children couldn't visit over the holidays. We said, "Merry Christmas" along with each goodbye, but as the afternoon wore on, I wasn't any closer to peace than when I had given in to hysteria that morning.

I was cold, the weather was miserable, and I couldn't see that we were making a difference in anyone's life. If we hadn't been delivering the groceries, someone else would have.

The last address was several miles south. Watching the snow swirl across the road, I started the car. The sooner we made this last delivery, the sooner we could get home and I could get warm. Some intangible wind seemed to be cutting through even the closely woven fibers of my new coat.

On the way, I steered with my left hand and groped for the address card. Glancing at the back, I noticed some handwritten words under the heading "Special Needs." That space had been blank on the other cards, but this one very plainly stated, "Large-size woman's coat."

Oh, fiddlesticks. I should have seen that before we left. I could have chosen a coat off the rack against the back wall. With the rush of the holidays, no one else from the Salvation Army would make a special trip way out here just to deliver a coat. And I certainly wasn't going to offer my own on such a cold afternoon, even though I wore the same size.

At last we arrived at the address on the card. Years ago, the place must have been a cute cottage. Now it was only a tired, leaning shack. Its graying boards still showed signs of white paint, undoubtedly applied many years ago. An old car sat in the yard—up on blocks and tireless. I wondered if they had

REFLECT

sold the tires to provide something else.

Jay and Holly had fallen asleep during the drive, but as I shut off the ignition, they sat up and looked around. "Gosh, Mom," was Jay's only comment as he looked toward the house.

When I had turned around from pulling the last bag of groceries from the back seat, an elderly woman solemnly gestured toward the back door. The front one was sealed with plastic to keep out December's subzero temperatures.

The three of us stomped our feet at the back steps as a man in his late seventies held the door for us. "Don't worry about the snow," he said. But still we stomped, perhaps stalling for time.

Once inside, I set the bag on the kitchen table, trying not to notice the worn-out room. Everything was clean, but only near the walls were any pieces of tile left. Those once in the middle of the room had been worn to the floorboards beneath. The curtains had been mended so many times the stitches made a pattern in the flimsy material.

The elderly couple thanked me repeatedly. All I had to do was smile and walk out the door. Instead, I found myself apologizing for not having brought a coat. The woman smoothed the sleeves of her old navy blue sweater and gave us an *it's okay* smile.

It struck me that she had been disappointed so many times that another disappointment hardly mattered. Through the curtains I could see the snow blowing across the frozen driveway. Suddenly I took off my coat and said, "Here, try this one on for the size."

She hesitated, then did as I asked. She even buttoned it and then smiled at her husband as she turned to show him the pleats on the back. It fit! I leaned forward to unpin the badge from the collar.

"Looks like you got yourself a coat," I stammered, afraid she wouldn't accept.

Instead, she hugged me and whispered, "God bless you, honey," as tears rolled down her cheeks.

Suddenly I was crying, too. What had been awkwardly offered was graciously accepted.

"Thank you for letting me do this," I whispered to her.

Her husband and Jay and Holly silently watched, not sure of what to do. Soon we were out the door, waving goodbye to the old couple standing together.

The Family Treasury of Great Holiday Ideas

As the door closed, Holly turned to me "Mom! It's freezing! And you gave away your coat!"

I felt like giggling.

"I know. Isn't it wonderful? Nobody needs two gray coats, anyway. And you know what? This is the warmest I've been all day!"

I gave Holly's shoulders a squeeze. Hysteria wouldn't threaten me again for a long time.

Sandra Picklesimer Aldrich
is the senior editor of Focus on the Family
magazine in Colorado Springs.

REAL CHRISTMAS JOY
(Deuteronomy 15:11)

Those new clothes I've been waiting for
I finally get to buy!
And I'm in such a festive mood,
For Christmas time is nigh.

The store is crowded while I shop,
But I don't mind a bit—
Arms full, I rush to try things on,
Wondering how they'll fit.

While walking past the twinkling lights
Hanging in the window
Something there draws my attention,
And my steps begin to slow . . .

A little face is pressed to the glass,
His eyes shining and bright—
My glance falls to his ragged coat,
And tears I have to fight.

REFLECT

He points to toys he cannot have
His lips are moving fast;
His mom looks sad as she takes his hand
And tries to pull him past . . .

All the things she cannot afford
But wishes that she could—
Her little boy deserves much more;
He's always been so good.

The clothes I hold seem heavy;
They weigh upon my arm—
And suddenly my shopping spree
Has lost all of its charm.

Laying aside the things I chose,
I hurry out the door,
Knowing that Jesus wants me to
Be generous to the poor.

I slip my gift into her hand
And feel my spirit soar . . .
For her eyes glisten as she leads
Her son into the store.

Denise A. DeWald
resides in
Au Gres, Michigan.

It was the day after Thanksgiving and I was plenty worried. I like Christmas, but not half as much as my mom does. She has a routine about Christmas that we stick to like glue.

On that Friday, we took down the Thanksgiving decorations, and Mom cleaned the house good. My brothers and I went outside to shoot baskets, just to stay out of her way.

That night I counted the money in my wallet again. I had bought presents a couple of days before. Dish towels for Mom, white socks for Dad, and nifty cars for my brothers. All I had left was forty-two cents. How had I forgotten about the stockings?

Saturday morning, after chores, we watched cartoons and waited for Mom to start the tradition. It wasn't long until she called me into the living room.

"Bring me the hammer from the kitchen toolbox, please."

I took it to her. I don't know why she doesn't get it before she starts stringing the wire across the fireplace for the stockings but she never does.

After a lot of pounding, she got the nails in the old holes and wrapped the wire around them.

"What do you think, Rob? Looks pretty festive."

"Sure does, Mom." I knew what she would say next. Maybe there will be something in them before nightfall.

"Maybe there will be something in them before nightfall," she said happily.

From the day after the day after Thanksgiving, when we hang the stockings, until Christmas Eve, we all sneak things into the stockings. Santa finishes filling them up when he comes. And all that time we never peek, but we get to feel through the socks and make guesses. Of course, nobody ever tells us if we're right or not.

Before lunch there was something in all the stockings, except Mom's. We all knew she had put the things in the socks but she wouldn't talk. I checked with the other boys and they didn't have anything for the stockings, either. By suppertime, there was one more thing in the stockings, except for Mom's. I thought I could feel a new pocketknife, but I couldn't be sure.

I knew Mom was feeling left out because there was nothing in

REFLECT

her stocking and it was almost time for Christmas cheer. While she was in the kitchen, I went upstairs to my room to think. What did I have to put in her stocking? She always said it was the thought that counts, but I didn't have many thoughts.

I looked through the drawers of my desk but didn't find anything that would work. Paper clips or pencils didn't seem right, neither did rubber bands or a ruler. Then I saw my feather collection.

I had collected feathers all summer and poked the ends into a short plastic tube I had found in the barn. I must have had thirty feathers and I loved their soft feel. They weren't just from our chickens, either. I had one from a cardinal and one from a blue jay. There were lots of different colors and shades. Mom might love them as much as I did.

I snuck down the stairs and stuffed my feather collection in Mom's stocking. Joe saw me.

"What are you doing? She'll hate that," he said.

"Why?"

"You know she's afraid of spiders and stuff."

"Feathers aren't spiders."

"No, but they're from birds, and I don't think she likes birds much either. She wouldn't let me get that parakeet I wanted."

I was going to take it out, but Mom came in the room as I reached for it.

Her eyes lit up when she saw her stocking. "Something in my stocking," she said and walked over to feel it. "Whatever can it be?" She felt and felt but said she had no idea what it was.

I looked at Joe and he looked at me. There was no way I could take it out now.

We had Christmas cheer in the living room. Mom filled the reindeer glasses with pop and brought in a tray of cookies. We all had our Christmas cheer by the fireplace so we could look at the stockings.

Two weeks later all the decorations were up. Every decoration my brothers and I had ever made in school was on the walls and we had decorated the Christmas tree. We had Christmas cheer with the lighting ceremony when Dad put the star on the top of the tree.

I had wrapped my presents and put them under the tree. By adding another two weeks' allowance to my money, I had

The Family Treasury of Great Holiday Ideas

enough to buy packs of gum to put in everybody's stocking—including my own, since I like gum. But I kept thinking about that feather collection. Maybe Joe was wrong. I loved it, so why wouldn't Mom?

Christmas morning finally came. First thing we did was light a fire and put on Christmas music while Mom plugged in the coffeepot. Then we tackled our stockings. I got that pocket-knife, just like I had wanted, and disappearing ink, gum, poster paints, gum, a new belt, two candy bars, gum, an apple, and an orange. What a haul.

"Rob."

I looked up when Mom said my name. She was holding my feather collection and looked like she was going to cry. She hated it. Joe was right, it was a dumb idea.

"Rob," she said again. "I will treasure your feather collection always. This is a gift from the heart, the most special kind. Thank you, Rob. I'll keep it in my desk and whenever you want to see it or add to it, you may."

She smiled at me with her eyes all shiny, and I will never forget that Christmas as long as I live.

Veda Boyd Jones
writes romance novels "that confirm my own
values." She lives in the Ozarks of Missouri
and is the author of Gentle Persuasion
(Heartsong Presents).

Lo, how a rose e'er blooming
From tender stem hath sprung,
Of Jesse's lineage coming,
As men of old have sung.
It came a floweret bright,
Amid the cold of winter
When half spent was the night.

German (15th century)

REFLECT

For several years I have written a poem to enclose with Christmas cards. Our cards are always sent with personal notes—a gift that can't be purchased.

The Father sent an invitation
To the rich and to the poor;
"Come attend a celebration
Like one never held before."

He had made a proclamation:
"I will send My Son in love,
To be your friend and Savior;
The Gift—One perfect—from above."

The joyous shouting of the angels,
"Praise to God and peace to men,"
Rings throughout the endless ages,
And we hear it now as then.

Jesus came to bring salvation
To the rich and to the poor.
Within our hearts a celebration—
Like we'd never known before.

Let us sing out with the angels,
"Praise to God and peace to men,"
For throughout eternal ages,
Celebrations will not end.

*Jeanne M. Roth
resides in
Sweet Home, Oregon.*

The Family Treasury of Great Holiday Ideas

For Christmas when I was eleven years old all I wanted was a Darling Debbie doll. Darling Debbie was dressed in a blue formal dress with silver threads running through the material. She wore high heels, a necklace, and pearl earrings in her pierced ears. She was the prettiest doll I had ever seen. Although the previous year my cousin had given me a long talk about Santa Claus, I still held on to the desire for Santa to prove himself once again.

We lived in Missouri at the time but we always went to Grandma and Grandpa's home for Christmas. When time came to load the car for the six-hour trip, I became Mother's helper. I was hoping for just a peek at a package large enough to accommodate a Darling Debbie doll. But there was not one. When we got to our destination again I helped, this time to unload the car, but still no doll.

On Christmas Eve morning the plans were changed. We left my grandparents' home and went to visit with an aunt and uncle. Guess who helped load all those things in the car again!

In the early hours of Christmas morning I got up and tiptoed to the bathroom (by way of the Christmas tree, of course!). Santa had already made his stop and there was a Darling Debbie Doll!

I whispered Mother's name until she answered and I told her what I had seen. She said, "Really? Well, it's too early to be up so go on back to bed before you wake the others." I went, but I could hardly wait for the others to get up.

I left Darling Debbie, which I renamed Merry Christmas, at home with Mother and Daddy as I went off to college.

Years later, for my thirty-fifth birthday, Mother and Daddy gave me Darling Debbie again. This time Mother had dressed her in a dress made of the same fabric as the bridesmaids' dresses at my wedding. The doll was in a cherry display case with a glass front. Daddy had made the display case from lumber cut from a cherry tree that grew on their farm.

Mother told me then that if, as a child, I had helped to load and unload our winter coats, I might have discovered the doll on the way to my grandparents' home.

Jane Richardson Holden
resides in
Marion, Mississippi.

REFLECT

Within the glow
of candlelight,
come peaceful thoughts
of that first night;
Of baby Jesus,
Precious One,
Who came to earth
as God's own Son.

His precious gift,
the gift of love,
was given to us
by God above;
Within my heart
I do believe
God's love is real—
I now receive.

Gayle Blair Urban
resides in
Woodbridge, Virginia.

Let all mortal flesh keep silence,
And with fear and trembling stand;
Ponder nothing earthly minded,
For with blessing in His hand,
Christ our God to earth descendeth,
Our full homage to demand.

From the Liturgy of St. James

The Family Treasury of Great Holiday Ideas

Some wise men saw a new and brilliant star
Which meant, they knew, a special child was born.
    They did not live in Galilee or Bethlehem—
They were not even Jews.
And yet they came from far off in the east,
By caravan, enduring danger, sand, and heat
    To find this child.
God chose wealthy men of wisdom from that distant land
But also nearby shepherds poor in this world's goods,
    As first to see His Son.
So let us all, from north, east, south, or west
Come rejoicing in the birthday of the King,
Who wants to be our Savior and our Lord,
    If we but choose.

Dorothy M. Harpster
resides in
Lewisburg, Pennsylvania.

My "Store-boughten" Christmas

Every Christmas of my life has been special. Our family looks forward to celebrating Christ's birth with our own family traditions. Although some of them have changed over the years many remain the same . . . the decorating, the joy, the delight in preparing surprises for all, from the smallest through the oldest.

But of all the Christmases I have had, one stands out in my memory. It was there I learned the meaning of giving. It was the "store-boughten" Christmas of long ago.

I was born in 1935, a time when money was scarce but love abundant in our home. We had plenty to eat and wear, a good warm home, but very little cash. And yet when Christmas came

REFLECT

all the relatives gathered at Grandma's. Somehow, year afte
year, my mother and aunts managed to find time and a littl
money to provide gifts from each to every other family mem
ber, and it usually ranged up to about thirty gifts! There wer
many hand-worked items, embroidered pillowcases, towel:
and so on. There were warm socks for the men and kitche
utensils for the women. It was a matter of planning almost fror
one Christmas to the next to be sure no one was left out. List
were checked and rechecked, to be sure that not one name ha
been omitted! Even the wrapping was a real challenge. Al
those gifts, carefully wrapped in last year's Christmas papei
saved and ironed out. Even today it hurts to see careless finger
tear eagerly into beautiful paper. We saved every scrap w
could then, and every inch of reusable ribbon.

Within our own immediate family, my two brothers and
painstakingly made the gifts for each other and for our folks.

But then came the year that made a change. I don't remembe
if I was eight or nine. But this year I wouldn't be making gift
for my family. This is the year my gifts were to be "store
boughten!" Never had a little girl been more thrilled than whe
we started out early one mid-December Saturday morning o
our annual Christmas shopping trip. It was fifty miles from ou
small hometown in the Cascade Mountains of Washington t
Everett, the "big town" that on our infrequent trips seeme
almost like fairyland. All those stores, big buildings, eleva
tors—they were wonderful!

Yet even they had lost their charm this day. My eyes wer
fastened on one area—the three large, ten-cent stores, Kresge':
Woolworth's, and Newberry's, all in the same block. They of
fered hours of shopping adventures to my brothers and me. W
were perfectly safe in them, and could wander freely while Da
and Mom took care of all the other gifts that must be bought. I
my sweaty hand, clutched inside my mitten, was a vast fortune
the means by which I was going to purchase my four gifts—a
entire dollar—one hundred pennies magically turned into fou
shining silver quarters! Never had anyone felt so rich as I di
that Saturday, dazzled by all the things the store offered.

Where should I start? I knew the value of that money. We al
had our usual chores at home. The boys carried wood an

The Family Treasury of Great Holiday Ideas

umped water. I helped in the house. But when we wanted to
rn a little money, there were always what we called the
windows-and-the-cupboards." Never had any family had
ch clean windows and cupboards! Five cents for washing one
rge section of windows, and there were six sections! Ten cents
r washing the cupboards! The money in my hand represented
any weeks of shining clean windows and cupboards. Not for
ything would I have spent any of that hard-earned money on
yself. It was for Dad, Mom, and the boys that I now felt such a
arm happiness at the thought of it.

Mom's gift was easy—and just the right price! It was the year
first saw artificial Christmas corsages. This one was wonder-
ul, with its holly and ribbon, even a tiny cone sprinkled with
itter to represent snow. And it cost exactly twenty-five cents!
knew that one dollar split into four presents must be twenty-
ve cents apiece. Next came my older brother's present. I can't
member what it was; I do remember it also cost exactly
venty-five cents. I also remember the pride and wonder that
y shopping was going so well. I had gone through each of the
ree stores only one time and already, after about two hours, I
d half my shopping done!

But then I hit a snag. On my way past a high counter I saw
hat I wanted for my little brother. It was beautiful. It was a
ank for him to put his pennies in, but oh, what a wonderful
ank it was. It was metal, a little monkey with a friendly
ainted grin, red jacket, blue pants, boots. But the best thing of
l was that when money was dropped in, the monkey tipped
s hat! I had to have it for my brother, I just had to have it!
olding my breath, I looked for the price tag . . . twenty-nine
ents. My heart sank. It was too much. I can't remember a more
uer childhood disappointment than when I saw that tag, four
nts over what I knew I had to spend. What could I do?

I finally turned away. If I spent twenty-nine cents on this,
en I would only have twenty-one cents for my dad's present.
was clear cut. I never once thought of finding my folks and
king them for the extra four cents; we didn't ask for things,
e knew our parents didn't have much. Dejected, near tears, I
alked away. I think I even went back into the other two stores
d looked again for something else—but ever in the back of

REFLECT

131

my mind was that little monkey and the jaunty way he tippe
his hat. Christmas would be spoiled. Why had I ever seen it if
couldn't get it for my little brother?

Who is to say that such childish disappointments are no
recognized by the Author of Christmas? I do not think it was
miracle—and yet, was it just a little more than chance that as
walked between the narrow aisles, my eyes lit on somethin
else? A display of bandannas, such as Dad used for handker
chiefs in his wood work. And they were twenty-one cents!
stood there staring, almost unable to believe my luck until th
lady said, "May I help you, little girl?"

I managed to mumble that I wanted a navy blue bandanna
and carefully watched while she counted out the change—th
four pennies that would go with my last quarter and buy tha
little monkey bank! There was no hesitating when I got them
Hurrying all the way back, I was so afraid it would be sold
What if it had been?

But it wasn't. The same little painted monkey face smiled jus
as warmly at me when I counted out the quarter and fou
pennies. It was mine!

When Christmas came and all the gifts were given out
watched my family. Each of them was so surprised, so happ
with their "store-boughten" gifts—but none so happy a
Randy. He loved that little bank. Someone gave him a few
pennies. He dropped them in, one at a time, watching th
monkey tip his hat, then turned the little release in the bottom
got his pennies out, and dropped them in again! I had spent
dollar, I had given everything I had, but I had gained a thou
sand dollars' worth of happiness.

The years have come and gone, over fifty of them, eac
bringing its own unique Christmas. The whole family n
longer gets together; it has grown too big. Yet every time I see
snowflake or go Christmas shopping, I look back to that firs
"store-boughten" Christmas.

I don't even remember what my own Christmas gift was tha
year. It wasn't important. What was important was the joy o
my family's faces when they saw what I had given them.

Perhaps because of that first "store-boughten" Christmas,
have never felt Christmas was too commercialized. I love th
preparation, the special services, the using of what I have to d

The Family Treasury of Great Holiday Ideas

the very best I can. The Wise Men came, bringing gifts. And on that first "store-boughten" Christmas I knew how they felt— and still do.

Colleen L. Reece,
author of such inspirational romance novels
as Candleshine *(Heartsong Presents),*
A Girl Named Cricket, and
The Hills of Hope (Barbour Books),
resides in Auburn, Washington.

JUST A STAR

Just a star
the distance seemed really far.
Yet by a star the wise men were led
to Bethlehem the House of Bread
leading to a stable
where Christ was born
on the day we call Christmas morn.

Just as the wise men followed the star
so we have a path to follow.
He has given us the light
much like the star so bright
so that even when day turns to night
we still have love, joy, and peace—
gifts given to us by God's only Son
so that His work in us be done.

Mary Jo Mougey
resides in
Union, Nebraska.

REFLECT

THE GIFT

Our greatest gift wasn't wrapped in fancy paper and bows.
It was given as a babe wrapped in swaddling clothes.
There was no Christmas tree with lights glittering
    and bright.
Yet the star of the east led to the everlasting light.
 . . . No Christmas carolers singing "Silent Night,"
But a heavenly host sending forth a great light.
 . . . No family and friends gathered 'round the table,
But a miraculous birth in the lowly stable.
Do you get lost in the rush this time of year?
Or remember the Savior and hold Him near?

Jan Capps
resides in
Raymond, Washington.

REFUGE

The snow in Judah
was not colder than
the heart of Herod.
But Egypt's rivers
warmed the small
king in exile,
where first palms
praised his quiet advent,
green hosannas for
a season's welcome.

Rosalie Marshall
resides in
La Grande, Oregon.

J— Jehovah Shalom, Prince of Peace
For unto us a child is born, unto us a Son is given: and the government shall be upon his shoulder: and his name shall be called Wonderful, Counselor, the Mighty God, the Everlasting Father, the Prince of Peace. (Shalom)

(Isaiah 9:6)

E— Everlasting Light
For mine eyes have seen thy salvation, which thou hast prepared before the face of all people; a *light* to lighten the Gentiles, and the glory of thy people Israel. (Luke 2:30-32)

S— Son of God
And she brought forth her firstborn son, and wrapped him in swaddling clothes, and laid him in a manger; because there was no room for them in the inn.   (Luke 2:7)

U— Us
S For unto you is born this day in the city of David a Savior, which is Christ the Lord.   (Luke 2:11)

Why?

For God so loved the world that he gave his only begotten son, that whosoever believeth in him should not perish, but have everlasting life.   (John 3:16)

Savior . . . For me . . . For you . . . .

Merry Christmas and Shalom (Peace) in Yeshua (Jesus)!

Carol Kirkelie
resides in
Canterbury, Connecticut.

REFLECT

God sent His love as a newborn child,
Who lay in a manger, so gentle and mild.
Angels announced the event of His birth,
All heaven rejoiced, when this Child came to earth.
As shepherds were tending their flocks that night,
The glory of the Lord shone 'round them so bright.
"Fear not," said an angel, "I bring glad tidings of joy."
Then they hastened to Bethlehem to gaze on this boy.
From out of the east came a bright shining star,
That guided the wise men from their country afar.
They came bearing gifts to the Christ-Child King,
As Christmas draws nigh, what will *you* bring?

Jan Capps
resides in
Raymond, Washington.

A BABY BOY

This is the holy season of goodwill, peace, and joy:
all because of the birth of a baby boy.
He was born in a stable outside of town:
when the Christ Child was born, the animals knelt down.
The shepherds in the fields were frightened by the light;
heavenly angels came to guide them safely through the night.
He came into the world in a simple humble way;
teaching us to love one another every day.
Goodwill, peace, and joy could be with us throughout
the year;
perhaps, if we listen, His joyful message we will hear.

Judith M. Perkins
resides in
Crown Point, Indiana.

The Family Treasury of Great Holiday Ideas

One of the leanest—and best—Christmases my children and I ever celebrated was in 1990—just after we moved from New York to Colorado Springs. I had thought our East Coast dwelling was sold, but as we drove across the country to our new home, the buyer had backed out. We arrived in the West to the news that I was now the not-so-proud owner of two dwellings. We had some tense moments financially—and even depleted the saving account to $34—but we managed, with God's help, to squeak by. Then Christmas loomed. I wondered how we were going to handle presents.

I had learned long ago that the greatest gift parents can give children is a pleasant memory. Jay and Holly didn't remember the expensive toys and intense decorating that had been part of their earlier holidays—when we'd been a two-salaried family before their dad died—but they did remember the midnight when we impulsively donned snowsuits over our pajamas to make snow angels on the front lawn.

I thought of the coupon books they made when they were in elementary school. I still have the one Holly assembled when she was seven. In large, wobbly printing, she promised to help me with grocery shopping and dust the low parts of the tables. Maybe I'll redeem those coupons when I'm ninety.

Well, it was time to go back to creativity. I still wanted—and needed—our new friends who were other single-parent families to come for Christmas dinner. But we were going to have to rethink our plans for gift giving. Thus, three weeks before Christmas, and over one of my inexpensive pasta dinners, I explained our financial crunch. My new friends—also single parents—were relieved at my suggestion that we'd exchange homemade items or gifts of service. We also agreed that we'd all see this as an adventure rather than "belt-tightening."

Christmas morning arrived under incredible Colorado blue skies! Our family time began with our own early morning gift exchange in which Jay gave Holly tickets for math help, and Holly promised to do several loads of his laundry. Jay's gift to me was a sheet of coupons for eight long walks together.

Taken from: *From One Single Mother to Another* by Sandra P. Aldrich. Copyright © 1991 Regal Books, Ventura, CA 93003. Use by permission

REFLECT

Holly's gift was a free-verse poem called "Parenting," in which she thanked me for being "a great person and mom."

Of course I cried when I read it. After all, many parents don't have things like that said about them until they're dead! Not having money forced the kids to come up with creative solutions to their problem and with ideas I hope they'll carry over into their future.

A few hours later, the other families arrived for dinner, each bringing a special dish to create a bountiful table. When it was time to open gifts, we exchanged promises for help with errands, plates of cookies, and delightful homemade gifts, including spray-painted avocado candlesticks. It was an incredible day—and all because we were determined not to let a lack of money spoil our fun.

Oh, the New York condo finally sold the spring after our arrival in Colorado, and we were able to start keeping Sears and J C Penney in business again. Amazingly, though, it is that Christmas of 1990 that we refer to as we share fun memories. What could have been a depressing time has now become the standard by which we measure family fun. Years from now, I'm convinced, Jay and Holly will be telling their own children about the year "Grandma Aldrich" got down to $34. I trust that what could have been a depressing story will become a family story of faith. After all, that's a remarkable Christmas present to pass along to the next generation.

Sandra Picklesimer Aldrich
and her children live in Colorado Springs,
Colorado, where she is the senior editor of
Focus on the Family *magazine.*

Christmas time is almost here
And people are excited.
They are making out their Christmas lists
So no one will be slighted.

They dig around the attic
To get the trimmings out,
Some of them are really old
That's when we all shout—

"Look, oh, look what I have found
This little tiny deer,
An angel, and a little sleigh,
And look, a Santa's here!"

We trim the tree and Mama bakes
She also wraps the gifts.
She's busy every single day
The workload never shifts.

Then comes Christmas morning
We go to church and sing
Thank You for the Christ Child
Our Savior and our King.

*Vi Werner
resides in
Chetek, Wisconsin.*

REFLECT

In a Bethlehem stable
A baby was born
To Joseph and Mary
That first Christmas morn.

They called him Emmanuel
Which means "God with us,"
For One who was holy
His birth caused no fuss.

But the angels in heaven
Rejoiced at His birth,
They knew that this baby
Was God here on earth.

He came with the purpose
To save sinful man,
And die to redeem us,
For no one else can.

A place up in heaven
Is waiting for all
Who believe in the Savior
And on His name call.

Our praise and our worship
To You, Lord, we bring,
For this Christmas baby,
Emmanuel, our King.

Glenna Fox
resides in
Coeur d' Alene, Idaho.

The Family Treasury of Great Holiday Ideas

Where I grew up there was never snow, not even a frost at Christmas time. Instead, the hot sun of a Queensland summer scorched the wheat stubble white in the paddocks on the flat, black soil plains of the Darling Downs. Some years the harvest time would be running so late that by Christmas Eve there would still be a few remaining acres to be reaped.

I particularly remember those years when the four of us would wait anxiously all day on Christmas Eve for our father to stop his frantic efforts to get the late harvest finished. But he always stopped work in time for us all to pile into the truck to get our Christmas tree.

This was no small venture. To buy one meant too long a trip on the rough roads into the nearest city, Toowoomba. No trees grew on the plains, so we had to drive some distance to find patches of scrub in the low lying hills.

Eagerly, we would search for a "real" Christmas tree, a pine tree with a pointed top. We often had to walk a long way from the gravel roads into the bush, always on the lookout for angry snakes in the long grass. Only a few times did we ever find that "real" tree, and even then it was never like the traditional dark green fir trees in our story books with the snow glistening on the boughs.

Usually we would end up back home with the only tree available, a small gum tree. A few times I remember having to end up with scraggly branches off large old trees that we would tie together with string to make it as busy as possible. The eucalyptus perfume would then invade the delicious smell of chickens cooking, sponge cakes, and the other delightful odors in Mum's kitchen on Christmas Eve.

Ah, but the sheer delight of decorating our tree! My wonderful mother's encouragement never failed. It was always "the very prettiest tree we've ever had!" And we never dared to forget to leave out some fruit and sweets for that special visitor who was expected that night.

But the best was yet to come on Christmas morning. Father Christmas always transformed it with parcels, balloons, handkerchiefs, and comics spread over branches, and all the large parcels piled in a heap around the red crepe-paper-covered

REFLECT

bucket holding the tree.

When I married my wonderful minister husband, he was used to a Santa Claus filling a pillow at the foot of his bed in an inner suburb in Sydney. Their only tree was a small artificial one set on a small table with a smattering of what I thought were rather boring, glittering decorations.

When we shared our very first Christmas with our first baby, there was a big decision to make. Would we buy an artificial tree to use every year? Would we go out into the bush and find our own tree to cut down? Or would we spend money to buy one of the traditional fir trees being sold the weeks beforehand?

I still dislike the thought of the same artificial tree each year, but Ray just hates chopping down a "poor little tree not fully grown."

But guess what? Down through the years our three children didn't think it seemed like Christmas if Dad didn't go searching for our "very own tree!" We've never lived on the plains, so we've never had to resort to a gum tree. But our pine trees still have very rarely looked like the traditional ones.

Even last year the large old Mexican pine tree in our backyard in the Hunter Valley of New South Wales lost a couple of branches . . . they made a wonderful tree! Sure, the tip bent over a long way. The angel perched there was in danger of falling for days, but she didn't. And on Christmas Day the branches and long pale green boughs were transformed by balloons, handkerchiefs, and magazines. Large parcels still hid the red bucket.

After all, it was *our* Christmas tree!

Mary Hawkins
lives in Maitland, Australia, and is the author
of the inspirational romance novel
Search for Tomorrow
(*Heartsong Presents*).

Christmas is so many things
To young and old alike,
Memories of other years gone by,
The glow on the face of a tiny tyke!

It's the smell of fresh cedar in the house,
The nose-tickling aroma of pumpkin pies,
Mother's humming of carols and hymns,
A mysterious twinkle in Daddy's eyes.

It's snow crunching underfoot as you go,
Taking homemade cookies to each friend,
It's the gift of yourself you gladly share,
With the greeting cards you send.

But, best of all, it's a token of love,
The Prince of Peace and Light—
Born in a lowly manger bed,
That long-ago Christmas night.

Nancy A. Fintel
resides in
Byron, Nebraska.

And there were in the same country shepherds abiding in the field, keeping watch over their flock by night. And, lo, the angel of the Lord came upon them, and the glory of the Lord shone round about them: and they were sore afraid. And the angel said unto them, Fear not: for, behold, I bring you good tidings of great joy, which shall be to all people. For unto you is born this day in the city of David a Saviour, which is Christ the Lord. And this shall be a sign unto you; Ye shall find the babe wrapped in swaddling clothes, lying in a manger.

(Luke 2:8-12, KJV)

REFLECT

Christmas is bright like the stripes
    on a candy cane.
It sounds like the music of powerful
    proud trumpets.
It tastes like oven-fresh cookies.
It smells like the scent of pine needles.
Christmas looks like the smiles
    on children's faces
    when they open that present
    they've always wanted.
It makes you feel cozy, warm, and joyful.

*Steven D. Picazo
(age 12) resides in
Springville, New York.*

THE MOMENT OF TRUTH

We became Christians when I was twenty-three with a six-year-old son, Kenny, and a little daughter, Laurie, three. We had taught them the Santa myth but when we learned to love and appreciate our blessed Savior we determined to tell them the truth as soon as we could rake up the courage.

It happened one Sunday morning in December when the kids had piled into our bed for a love-in and free-for-all. We looked at each other and nodded. There'd never be a better time to tell them the heart-breaking news.

My kind husband began the story. "Do you remember how much Jesus loves you?" he asked.

"Yes!" Laurie replied. "More than the whole world."

"Even more than you love us," Kenny added.

"And do you know all the good things He gives us? Not only at Christmas but all the time?"

"Yes," Kenny screamed, loving the game. "He gives us flowers and trees. Blue sky and snow. I love snow."

The Family Treasury of Great Holiday Ideas

"He gave us Duke, too," Laurie yelled, not to be outdone. Duke was our magnificent collie dog.

"Right," my quaking husband said, obviously unable to tell them the crushing news. Would they ever believe anything we told them again? When his eyes met mine, pleading, I decided I'd do it.

But how?

"There really isn't any Santa Claus," I blurted out. "Just Daddy and me, and especially our precious Jesus."

The kids flopped onto pillows to think this over. After a moment Kenny said, "Oh. When is breakfast going to be ready?" Laurie forgot all about Santa Claus in her eagerness for breakfast. Those two kids never mentioned the name Santa Claus again.

VeraLee Wiggins
is the author of many inspirational romances,
including Sweet Shelter *and* Llama Lady
(Heartsong Presents).
She resides in Washington State.

Christmas Is Jesus

Is it Christmas when the tree is up and mistletoe is in each doorway? Is it Christmas when the mantel is adorned with candles and evergreen boughs and the house is filled with fragrant smells? Does Christmas happen when every shopping list has been filled and everybody's favorite new toys have been purchased and wrapped?

The holiday season does have an abundance of colorful sights, bustling sounds, and hectic schedules as we hasten to *do* all the things that we think *must* be done before Christmas arrives. "Where's the cranberry bread? It's not Christmas without the cranberry bread!" And, "What about another present for Dad? It's not right if Mom gets three and he gets only two! Let's run to the store!"

But Christmas doesn't come from the store. It can't be bought

REFLECT

at the five-and-dime. Christmas is more than that. Christmas is hugs from the heart, happiness shared, hope in all things— Christmas is Jesus. And Jesus is here for all mankind, today and always.

Gayle Blair Urban
resides in
Woodbridge, Virginia.

PRECIOUS ONE

Of sailors and shepherds
Of captains and kings
No human conceived
What this Child brings.

With hands clasped together
His face in repose
His lips somewhat puckered
Looking much like a rose.

Wise sages and lowly common men
Bowing down all through time
Still never knowing or dreaming
What God had in mind.

Sheila Hudson
resides in
Athens, Georgia.

I hoped for one thing that Christmas—to receive a sled, and it didn't even have to be *mine*. As the youngest of three girls with only two sleds, it seemed I was always waiting for my chance to ride.

And there it was under the tree on Christmas morning: an extra-long, varnished to a shine, Lightning Glider, just like the picture in the Sears catalogue! It was a gift to all of us and I wouldn't get to use it much, but now when Lois and Alice went squealing down the slope beside the barn or the steeper one across the creek and past the spring house, I'd be with them.

Mother reminded us, "Before anything else, we must visit Uncle at the hospital." We protested and pleaded, but not because we did not love the elderly man who'd come to live with us because he had neither home nor money. He had become part of our family, closer than most relatives.

But today was *Christmas*. There was new-fallen snow on the ground and we had just been given our new sled!

Wrapped gifts for Uncle sat upon the floor of our old Ford and Mother carried homemade treats. She and Dad got us singing carols and fun songs, to get our minds off our disappointment, and also so we would not worry about what we'd find. I had not seen Uncle since his leg was amputated, and my too vivid imagination had conjured monstrous possibilities.

Uncle cried when we came into his room, but he assured us these were tears of happiness. As he introduced us to the others in his ward, none of whom had visitors that Christmas morning, I was really glad we'd come.

That sled's now used by grandchildren, but the memory of our Christmas shared with Uncle is still part of me. At Christmas, Easter, Thanksgiving, and other holidays, we always include lonely or forgotten people in our festivities and happiness.

Eileen M. Berger,
known for her inspirational romance stories,
is the author of Lexi's Nature *and*
Tori's Masquerade *(Barbour Books) as well*
as Escort Homeward *and* A Place to Call
Home *(Heartsong Presents).*

REFLECT

Christmas fun is here to stay,
For Christmas fun should be in every day.
At all times we should thank God for His birth,
He showed us His love when He came to earth,
No longer is He a babe resting in a bed of hay,
Read the Bible and see that He is the only Way
To inner peace and Christmas fun all year 'round,
Invite Him into your heart and become heaven bound.

Lynne Gould
resides in
West Warwick, Rhode Island.

REASON FOR THE SEASON

'Tis Christmas Eve and all is still,
Santa rides o'er vale and hill.
Another Christmas now to heist,
But he is met by Jesus Christ!

"Old fellow, listen as I speak,
The kids might go on week by week,
Revering you, symbolically,
As they take down their Christmas tree.

'Tis *Christ*mas not *Santa*mas, hear
Do you intend to interfere?
Let it be known that this is treason,
I'm the reason for the season!"

Andrew J. Picazo
(age 11)
resides in
Springville, New York.

The Family Treasury of Great Holiday Ideas

Tinsel. Ribbon. Colored paper ripped and strewn everywhere. Shining-eyed children surrounded by a wealth of Christmas treasure. Yet I was not seeing those three children in the midst of yuletide plenty—I was remembering another three children from another time, almost fifty years ago; three children whose greatest Christmas treasure was the gift of wishing.

Every year it was the same. About the middle of November IT came, and a few days later THE OTHER ONE followed. Stuffed in our rural route mailbox, the "Sears and Sawbuck" and "Monkey Wards" Christmas catalogues were the open door to every dream.

"I get the Christmas catalogue!" How many times we squabbled over who got it first, when chores were done for the night—water pumped fresh, wood piled high in the woodbox! Once a "wish book" was in our possession, the rest of the world could go by—we'd never miss it.

I suppose today's psychologists would throw up their hands in horror at the way our parents encouraged us to dream over those wish books. "Why, you mustn't teach children to long for the things they can't have!"

Who cared? We knew it was unlikely we could get any of the things we picked out . . . but always there was that "someday" feeling.

Money was never plentiful and sometimes downright lacking, but the treasures of our hours with the wish books and their wonder could never be bought or taken away.

We made long lists, carefully writing down the page numbers, circling the items, then going back and crossing them all out to make new lists, with new items! Every minute with the wish book was, somehow, like actually possessing the things we longed for at the moment.

At last came Christmas Eve, THE NIGHT. The tree we gathered around had no lights—we had no electricity. But lamplight from the buffet top, shining on silver icicles and decorated tin cans, was beautiful.

We had no lighted star on top—but the Christmas angel perched on our tree smiled down at us. She, too, was beautiful.

One by one the gifts were given out. Our rule was that one

REFLECT

gift must be opened, so everyone could see, before the next one was given. There was no wanton ripping into packages. They were tied with curling ribbon, which was carefully untied and saved; and every piece of Christmas paper was handled gently I remember too well our "Christmas paper box," containing paper from years past that had carefully been ironed out with the "sad irons" heated on our wood stove. Any paper not saved could mean a shortage the next Christmas. The smaller packages came first. Always there were warm socks, sometimes mittens, the merely practical things we needed, but now somehow glorified by being under our Christmas tree.

Other gifts were pencils and color crayons, Prince Albert in a can for Dad, watercolors and "sticks and wheels," also known as Tinkertoys, for the children. Usually there was a sweater for at least one of the family, or flannel pajamas bright with colors, or a warm bathrobe. A country that could produce six feet of snow and -20° weather demanded such things. But, always, Mom and Dad found a little money, somewhere, so that there would be "fun" things, as well as the necessities.

Some Christmases were memorable because of a "big" present—the red wagon for my brother, a whole box of books for Dad—and, when I was only three or four, the biggest, most beautiful doll I had ever seen, for me!

As we grew older, the wish books remained important. Living in a small town had some disadvantages in shopping. With piggy banks and worried frowns, we used the wish books to order gifts for each other. Never was anything watched so intently as the mailbox out by the road, just visible through our stand of trees. Big packages were leaned up against the post, and had to be brought in from the weather as soon as possible We dreaded the printed letters which informed us that a particular something was "temporarily out of stock"; I remember a few times when a back-order present just didn't get there on time. But my resourceful mom overcame that—she simply cut the appropriate picture from the wish book, put it in a small box, then carefully disguised it by wrapping it in a much larger box, sometimes even adding something heavy to give it weight, and made it the prettiest package on the tree!

Now as I look back I realize what it was that made those Christmases happy, so filled with surprise and joy. We had had

The Family Treasury of Great Holiday Ideas

so much pleasure with OUR wish books and our lists, the anticipation and the secret planning, Christmas was what it should be—a time of rejoicing with each other over whatever the day brought.

I can still see three tousled heads bent over grimy paper, stubby yellow pencils writing down long lists of all the wonderful things from the wish book.

Most of the things we longed for and possessed only in imagination then have come now, in abundance. It is no longer necessary to count and frown over pennies. It is no longer necessary to weigh one gift over another, not by worth, but by how much it costs. But I can't help but wonder if somewhere along the way we've lost more than we've gained. Has the satisfaction of fulfillment really filled the space in our hearts once held by the wonder of wishing?

November comes—and with it the Christmas wish books. They are bigger now, filled with more expensive things to dream over.

At Christmas, when we all gather around a tree piled with packages, I can't help but wonder again—whose blessings are greater, those who give, those who receive, or those who once knew and enjoyed a different gift—the gift of wishing?

Colleen L. Reece,
an inspirational romance novelist, is also a
part-time teacher of creative writing. She lives
in Washington State and is the author of
Whispers in the Wilderness
(Heartsong Presents).

REFLECT

Christmas is a time for cheer,
a time to gather loved ones near.
A time to think about the past,
and know these memories will always last.

The joy that you see in those great big eyes,
when under the tree is that special surprise.
The warmth in your heart, like a fire aglow,
As you cherish the moments, too soon they will go.

So gather all your loved ones near,
while there's still time, and they are here.
The years fly by and soon are gone,
Leaving only memories to dream upon.

Remember that loved one, the babe in your arms,
the child under foot, the young girl with her charms.
The woman or man with the graying white hair,
they all are a part of the ones you hold dear.

Yes! No matter what your age may be,
there's time ahead to build memories.
So love each moment of this time of year,
make it filled with gladness, taking time to care.

Ruthie Knight
resides in
Pioneertown, California.

What is Christmas, it is quite mysterious;
    is it fun or is it serious?
Since when a child, I've seen the signs,
    the lights, the bells, and heard the chimes.
I've wakened early on this day
    with dreams of toys to open and play.
A chubby man in red and white.
    has brought them, I'm told, on a cold winter's flight.
And so through the years I've carried the spirit,
    and repeated this story for my own two to hear it.
But like some parents before me I've left out a part,
    that deals with creation and love from the heart.
For on this day a Child was born,
    He had no toys nor clothes to be worn.
So this season, let's all stop and praise,
    that little Child born on that day.
For this is Christmas, real and true,
    His gift is love for me and you.

William Sheehan
resides in
Brick, New Jersey.

What Child is this, who, laid to rest,
On Mary's lap is sleeping?
Whom angels greet with anthems sweet,
While shepherds watch are keeping?

Why lies He in such mean estate
Where ox and ass are feeding?
Good Christian, fear: for sinners here
The silent Word is pleading.

William C. Dix

REFLECT

A day of setting up our tree,
a day I thought would merely be
"perfection," but instead had noise
and real-live jostling ("watch this!") boys.
But now it's quiet,
bedtime fell . . .
they're all asleep,
my house is still.
And as I gaze on twinkling lights,
upon a tree that's soft and right,
I say a prayer for my three boys
and see there's love between the noise.

Gayle Blair Urban
resides in
Woodbridge, Virginia.

CHRISTMAS WITH GRAMMA

When I was a little girl, my grandmother made every Christmas special for my sister Gail and me. Opening our gifts on Christmas Eve was a tradition with us, and we looked forward to it with eagerness.

Not only did "Gramma" have a lot of beautifully wrapped presents under the tree, but she also made us wait until exactly six o'clock in the evening to open them—not a second before or after. The waiting was unbearable but oh, so exciting! I can remember many times standing before her old-fashioned black-and-white kitchen clock, when it was still five minutes 'til six, watching the second hand make its agonizingly slow trips around the clock, until it was finally six o'clock on the dot!

As soon as Gail and I saw that it was time to open our presents, we jumped up and down, squealed, and ran into the cozy woodstove-warmed living room, where the only lights burning were those coming from the big Christmas tree.

The Family Treasury of Great Holiday Ideas

Gramma was always the one to pass out the presents, and that seemed right somehow. Gail and I sat as close to the tree as we could, wondering who was going to get the first present. It seemed to take forever for Gramma to reach in and grasp that first package. I can still hear the way the wrapping paper crackled as her fingers closed around it.

And then . . . "To Gail!" At that Gail leapt up and took her first Christmas gift of the night from the grandmother we both loved so much.

As we both opened our gifts that Christmas Eve night, getting toy after toy that we had asked for all year, we knew in our hearts that we would never forget this wonderful "gramma" of ours, no matter how old we got, for the most important gift she gave us was love.

Denise A. DeWald
resides in
Au Gres, Michigan.

THE BEST GIFT
Thanks be unto God for his unspeakable gift.

(2 Corinthians 9:15)

> My gift
> Ornately wrapped
> tied in shiny ribbon
> Hastily laid
> Beneath a star-topped
> Artificial tree.
>
> His gift
> Simply wrapped
> in bands of cloth
> Beneath a star-studded
> Universe.

Brenda M. Picazo
resides in
Springville, New York.

R E F L E C T

Little baby, precious one,
God the Father's only Son,
Sent to earth that we might see,
Our hope for all eternity.

Little baby, meek and mild,
Mother Mary's first-born child.
Prophets foretold the virgin birth,
That God, Himself, would come to earth.

Baby Jesus, blessed Lamb,
Also called the great I AM,
Who but You could pay the price?
For man's sin were You sacrificed.

Little babe, draw us to You,
And cause our hearts to be renewed,
That we may live in heaven above,
The offspring of God's perfect love.

Oh Holy One, our mighty King,
To You, we let our praises ring,
And humbly on our knees we pray,
To thank You, God, for Christmas Day.

Glenna Fox
resides in
Coeur d'Alene, Idaho.

Note: The following was written by my grandmother, Nancy Goodman of Celeste, Texas. Shortly after this she had a stroke and now almost ten years later types with one hand as she writes stories of her childhood.

When I was a small child, I remember one Christmas as being very special. Being one of the younger of fifteen children, I remember Christmas because all of my older brothers and sisters would come home for the holidays.

On this special Christmas my mother was preparing the food and my brothers and sisters had arrived with their families. The whole house was filled with a sweet aroma that only family and Christmas can bring. As we sat down to eat our dinner, a knock was heard at the door. When my dad opened the door there stood a man needing food. It was very cold, and as this was in the 1930s, transportation was limited. He was trying to get home to his family and had missed the last train. He had started walking home and was cold and tired.

As the family looked at each other from across the dinner table, we knew he had to join us. We gave him the best we had but of course he was in a hurry to be with his family. I remember that Christmas as one of the most important in my childhood home because we helped a man that was really in need of food and a friend.

Inasmuch as ye have done it unto one of the least of these my brethren, ye have done it unto me. (Matthew 25:40)

Michael Goodman
resides in
Corpus Christi, Texas.

REFLECT

The candles all are lighted
A hush has filled the air
Where all was dark
Now all is bright
As we pass the spark around.

Likewise we must take
The love that Jesus gives to us
And pass it to our neighbor
To sow the seed of hope
In this world that once was lost.

Janet J. Henson
resides in
Middletown, Delaware.

O little town of Bethlehem,
How still we see thee lie;
Above thy deep and dreamless sleep
The silent stars go by.
Yet in thy dark streets shineth
The everlasting Light;
The hopes and fears of all the years
Are met in thee tonight.

Phillips Brook

It's shining lights and trees aglow,
It's Jesus' birthday, don't you know?

Scurrying for those gifts that win,
What fine gift are you giving Him?

"What does He want?" you ask of me,
Let's make a list and let us see.

He wants our aid to feed the poor,
To help the blind and heal the sore.

He wants our help to spread the Word,
Until the whole wide world had heard.

He gives us all the cash we earn,
He asks but for a small return.

He wants us to bring in those we see,
He'll save their souls eternally.

To be a friend to man and beast,
To share your good and bring relief.

He wants our love, our lives, our loyalty,
Lay down these gifts for Him beneath your tree.

He gave His life for you and me
What will you give to Him?

Mary Saunders
resides in
Orlando, Florida.

R E F L E C T

The land was taxed,
To their dismay—
But that was God's plan,
We know it today !

They went to be taxed—
Mary's baby was due,
But that was part
Of God's perfect plan, too!

There was no room
In any inn,
But a stable was the place
God provided for them.

Then Jesus was born—
In a manger He slept,
In the place where the straw
For the cattle was kept.

Wise men would come—
And a star shining bright,
Was the guide to the Christ Child
That first Christmas night.

Shepherds came—
To worship and pray,
"Glory to God!"
They heard angels say.

So as you go about
Your holiday with joy,
Remember God's Son,
The Holy Baby Boy!

Rachel Bell
(age 10) resides in
Shinglehouse, Pennsylvania.

The Family Treasury of Great Holiday Ideas

Snow falls softly to the ground,
as the family gathers 'round.

Outside carolers sing sweet melodies,
while the fire crackles quietly.

Pink and blue and soft white lace,
decorate our tree with grace.

Crisp wrapped gifts lie 'neath the tree,
waiting for me and my family.

As you take and light your tree,
do not forget how this day came to be.

One starry night, not long ago,
a baby came to Mary and her husband, Joe.

Many years later, it happens to be,
Jesus gave His life for you and me.

So as you celebrate with Christmas cheer,
and you open up your gifts this year,

Keep in mind, that Jesus Christ, God's only Son,
is the only perfect One.

Melissa Brooker
resides in
Warren, Pennsylvania.

REFLECT

Darkness was falling as we headed down the long country road with our freshly dug Christmas tree. With only a week until Christmas we were anxious about the upcoming holiday with our newborn son. Just before reaching home, we saw a car stopped with its headlights shining on what appeared to be a dog lying on the side of the road. Having two English setters ourselves, my husband Jim stopped our car and got out. The small dog had been hit and left to die. Inside the parked car was a couple who were passing by and had seen the injured dog but were unsure how to help.

Jim checked the dog for injuries while I ran to a nearby house where a new family had just moved in. I knocked on the door and was told to enter. A woman and two small children were counting pennies at the kitchen table. I asked if they had a dog and I gave a description of the injured animal. The children gasped and started crying for "Pebbles." The woman told me that the dog had just had a litter of six puppies four days ago. Her husband and I made our way back to the dog.

Pebbles was bleeding from the mouth and barely breathing. Both back legs were distended and one of her eyes was partially out of its socket. We managed to place the dog in a large flat pan we had for our tree and the family took it and the six puppies to a local veterinarian. The vet fed the pups and showed the family how to care for them while Pebbles stayed in his care.

Pebbles survived. She lost her eye but she recuperated enough to come home several days later. Her remarkable maternal instinct drove her to overcome her afflictions quickly.

The doctor's bill came to over $200, which was all the money the family had. They told the children Pebbles was their Christmas present and there would be no other gifts that year.

Volunteer workers from a humane society in a nearby town heard about this family who had sacrificed their Christmas for a dog. To show the family how much they appreciated their kindness and love, they secretly collected money and gifts for them.

Two days before Christmas a humane society volunteer asked me where the family lived. She had brought food, presents, toys, a turkey, dog food, and a portable heater for the family. They even had called the vet and explained the situa-

The Family Treasury of Great Holiday Ideas

tion to him. He then made all of Pebbles's further visits free of charge as his gift. When the children saw the volunteer bringing gifts into their home, they couldn't believe it. They screamed with joy and jumped up and down saying how happy they were to have Christmas.

My husband and I felt so blessed that year to truly see the spirit of Christmas living in today's fast-paced world.

Dana Walz
resides in
Bargaintown, New Jersey.

CHRISTMAS BABY

A star to lead the wise men
To the stable where He lay
Shepherds heard from angels
There's a baby in the hay.

Heaven and earth rejoicing
At this miracle of love
Mary smiling sweetly
At this baby from above.

He lay there in the manger
Kept warm from mother's care
But all the world would one day know
His Father laid Him there.

His love is never ending
His peace beyond compare
Such a tiny baby
Such a cross to bear.

Aimee Nicole Lillie
resides in
Marenisco, Michigan.

REFLECT

The learned wise men
Studied signs
And they knew.

While unlearned shepherds
Heard voices
And they knew.

To each is given
God makes known
And we wait.

The signs are given
Voices heard
Come anew.

Oh, come Lord Jesus
Even so
Thank You, Lord.

Janet J. Henson
is the daughter of Jocelyn P. Jamison
who resides in Middletown, Delaware.

And thou Bethlehem, in the land of Juda, art not the least
among the princes of Juda: for out of thee shall come a Gover-
nor, that shall rule my people Israel. Then Herod, when he had
privily called the wise men, enquired of them diligently what
time the star appeared.

(Matthew 2:6-7, KJV.

Just as parables were used to clarify the Kingdom of God, so too motion pictures, can teach, entertain, nourish, and upon occasion, even remind the viewer of the true significance of Christmas Day.

Ecclesiastes, chapter three states, "To every thing there is a season, and a time for every purpose . . . a time to weep, and a time to laugh; a time to mourn, and a time to dance." I'd say that justifies a time for entertainment. But let's keep Philippians 4:8 in mind when searching for videos: "Finally, brethren, whatsoever things are true, whatsoever things are honest, whatsoever things are just, whatsoever things are pure, whatsoever things are lovely, whatsoever things are of good report; if there be any virtue, and if there be any praise, think on these things." The following list contains holiday movies for each member of the family. Some contain a strong Gospel message, others edify, and then there are those that simply entertain. I do not suggest that these are the only well-made holiday films, but certainly they are among the finest.

Enjoy and Merry Christmas!

FOR THE LITTLE ONES

A Charlie Brown Christmas (1965) A perfect animated tale by Charles Schultz with the "Peanuts" gang searching for the true meaning of Christmas. Great dialogue, charismatic voice performances, and an award-winning jazzy score by Vince Guaraldi. How often do you hear cartoon heroes quoting from the Gospel of Luke, proclaiming the Christ-Child as the Messiah?

The Little Drummer Boy (1968) The very moving seasonal song comes to animated life with the capable voices of Greer Garson, José Ferrer, and Teddy Eccles. Puts present-giving in perspective.

Mr. Magoo's Christmas Carol (1962) You put Jim Backus together with Dickens's timeless classic, then add the Broadway talents of Jule Styne and Bob Merrill, and you're bound to have entertainment fit for the kid in all of us. Now don't tell anybody this, but I've watched this little gem each year since it first premiered, even once or twice in July!

REFLECT

The Other Wisemen Also animated, this charming narrative has been adapted for children. It tells the story of a man seeking the birthplace of Jesus but, because of his duty to others, he is delayed in the desert for thirty-three years only to see the Savior as He is being crucified. Hard to find; check your local Christian bookstore.

The Stable Boy's Christmas (1979) Danielle Brisebois, Darleen Carr, Sparky Marcus, and several of Hollywood's best character actors lend their talents to this Emmy-winning twenty-seven-minute TV special concerning a selfish young girl who learns a great lesson about the Christmas season from a figurine that comes to life. Soon we are transported to the night of Christ's birth where we witness the Savior's effect on the people of Bethlehem. Not in the same league as the others mentioned in this category, but like *The Little Drummer Boy*, it helps put present-giving in perspective.

The Greatest Adventure, The Nativity Hanna-Barbera's animated video series explores the lives of biblical heroes, including this version of the birth of Christ. Entertaining and educational. Also in the collection, *The Easter Story*, as seen through the eyes of three young visitors from the twentieth century.

FOR THE FAMILY

When it comes to the famous Dickens tale, here are three of the best renditions: *A Christmas Carol* (1951) starring Alastair Sim; *A Christmas Carol* (1984) with George C. Scott; and the musical version, *Scrooge* (1970) with Albert Finney. Each a well-acted parable with regard to redemption.

Here are two corny old chestnuts for you, but with the music of Irving Berlin and the enchantment of Astaire, Crosby, and Kaye, you're destined to have a good time. *Holiday Inn* (1942) stars Bing Crosby and Fred Astaire in a romantic triangle about a crooner opening a dinner theatre on holidays only. *White Christmas* (1954) stars Bing Crosby, Danny Kaye, Rosemary Clooney, and Vera-Ellen. Two song and dance men travel to Vermont during a snowless yuletide season in order to help both a struggling sister act and their wartime commanding officer. Will Crosby win over Clooney? Will the resort be saved? Will it snow on Christmas Eve?

The Family Treasury of Great Holiday Ideas

Three Godfathers (1948) John Wayne, Pedro Armendariz, and Harry Carey, Jr. Three outlaws, running from a posse, come across a dying woman and her newborn baby. The symbolism between the Christ Child and this new foundling has a redemptive effect on the three bandits. Sincere performances, beautiful cinematography, and the skillful direction of John Ford highlight this insightful western.

Jesus of Nazareth (1977) Franco Zefferelli's epic production of the life of Christ. Considered by many to be the best film about the Son of Man, *Jesus of Nazareth* is acclaimed for its thorough biblical and historical research. A very moving and spiritual experience, with many memorable performances including those of Robert Powell, Anne Bancroft, Ernest Borgnine, and Laurence Olivier. Its length (371 min.) will take several evenings to digest, but I highly recommend the effort.

FOR MATURE VIEWERS

The Gathering (1977) with Ed Asner and Maureen Stapleton. This Emmy-winning TV movie focuses on a dying man's efforts to reunite his family. It reinforces the importance of family and presents positive Christian images including a believable prayer, the Scripture reading of Jesus' birth, and a child's baptism. Forget the sequel.

The Bishop's Wife (1947) A debonair angel attempts to help a frustrated pastor and his neglected wife. Cary Grant, Loretta Young, David Niven—you can't get any classier than those players!

A Christmas without Snow (1980) Made for TV movie about a woman (Michael Learned) who becomes involved with the members of her church choir and its perfectionist director (John Houseman).

Christmas Eve (1986) Loretta Young, Ron Leibman, and Trevor Howard head a seasoned cast in an account of an elderly woman trying to bring her grandchildren and their father back together. Young had not made a film in twenty-three years, yet proved she was still glamorous and gifted.

The Robe (1953) Based upon the Lloyd C. Douglas novel about a Roman centurion who wins Christ's robe in a dice game. Soon his life, and that of his slave, are changed as they discover Jesus

REFLECT

to be the Savior of the world. We see Jesus through the use of long shots and camera angles that focus the attention not on an actor portraying Christ, but on the people who came into His presence. This method was effectively used, giving the story a great dignity. Richard Burton was nominated for an Oscar, but Victor Mature steals the picture with a moving performance as the converted slave, Demetrius. The depiction of the early church and the life-changing power of our Lord make this film worth viewing.

The Scarlet and the Black (1983) Made for TV. True story of a priest (Gregory Peck) who harbored allied POW escapees and the Nazi official (Christopher Plummer) who tries to catch him. The film has little to do with the Christmas season other than the examination of a man whose life was affected by Christ. The film is a bit long (155 min.) but the message contained at the end of the picture should not be missed. A true example of Jesus' compassion will help remind each of us to love our enemies.

A CLASSIC FOR ALL TIME

It's a Wonderful Life (1946) I know, I know, we've all seen it a million times, but I believe it is one of the most important films Hollywood ever produced. James Stewart is given the opportunity to see what his community would have been like if he had never been born. He reminds us that we touch so many lives and can have a real influence on those lives. Full of Christian symbolism, *It's A Wonderful Life* reinforces the belief that our compassion and responsibility do make a difference in the lives of those with whom we come in contact. Director Frank Capra has given the world a great gift with this Christmas classic.

NOT YET ON VIDEO

The Holly and the Ivy Sir Ralph Richardson heads a capable English cast in this story of a dysfunctional family brought together in a remote Norfolk rectory. This well-acted British film is not yet on video. It usually airs at around three o'clock in the morning on local TV stations during the Christmas season. Might I suggest you tape it? It's worth the effort.

GREAT GIFT IDEAS

Shadowlands (1985) Joss Ackland and Claire Bloom. Award-winning film spotlighting the friendship and eventual marriage of English author C. S. Lewis to an American woman who discovers she is dying. A lovely picture that deals with the loss of a loved one.

Cotton Patch Gospel (1988) This is an excellent video for teens and adults. A musical/comedy/drama placing the Gospel of Matthew in modern-day Georgia. Funny, moving, inspirational. Contact your local Christian bookstore and ask them to order it (distributed by The Bridgestone Production Group). One of the most inspiring treatments of the New Testament I've seen on video. Great music by the late Harry Chapin. Truly a joy to watch, and appropriate for members of any denomination. My highest recommendation.

Babette's Feast (1987) Based on a short story by Isak Dinesen *(Out of Africa)* about two sisters in a small Danish town who take in a homeless woman as their servant. A beautiful story of devotion and sacrifice, urging us not to hide behind our religion but to put it into action. Winner of the Best Foreign Film of that year, with easy-to-read subtitles, it should not be missed— more like viewing a fine old painting or enjoying a sumptuous meal. American filmmakers could take a lesson from this remarkable film. Most video stores carry this one in the foreign film section.

Inn of the Sixth Happiness (1958) Ingrid Bergman stars in this moving true account of a missionary who leads a group of children on a perilous journey through pre-World War II China. Contains perhaps the best conversion scene I have viewed in such movies, as we witness the change in a man's life due to this remarkable woman's example. Christian viewers will be reminded that our lifestyle does greatly affect others.

Phil Boatwright
is the editor and film reviewer for
The Monthly Reporter, *a monthly*
newsletter, and author of
The Movie Reporter,
How to Choose a Good Video Every Time
(Barbour Books).

REFLECT

Christ was born on Christmas Day,
wreathe the holly, twine the bay,
Christus natus hodie;
the Babe, the Son, the Holy One of Mary.

Anonymous

REMEMBER

*A Treasury
of Holiday Traditions*

CONTENTS

Traditions to Make

THANKFUL HANDS

On Thanksgiving we put a paper-cut handprint, in the form of a praying hand, on each plate set at the dinner table. Each handprint has the name of one of our guests on it. We put this name face down. During Thanksgiving dinner we take turns telling why we are thankful for the person whose name appears on our handprint.

A GINGERBREAD STABLE

Because my husband is German we make gingerbread houses at Christmastime. However, last year we made a gingerbread stable, baby Jesus, Mary, Joseph, and the animals instead. I think the children enjoyed making this one even more. My husband's German heritage as well as our Christian heritage were celebrated at once.

Julie Grunwald
resides in
Tucson, Arizona.

So bring Him incense, gold, and myrrh,
Come peasant, King, to own Him:
The King of Kings salvation brings,
Let loving hearts enthrone Him.

William C. Dix

REMEMBER

A Humble Tree

My husband and I live in a small trailer. We tried using artificial trees and live cedar and pine trees for Christmas trees, but had problems with them for various reasons (cost and pine needles, cedar prickles stuck in our carpet, to name a few). We decided to start our own tradition, our "Charlie Brown" Christmas tree. We cut the top off a maple or similar tree, the kind with no leaves. We take small white tree lights and wrap them around the branches from top to bottom. We have also created theme Christmas trees by using just bows, or just glass ornaments. With no greenery on the tree, the white twinkling lights really make the tree decorations stand out. Also, by just cutting the top off the tree, the tree continues to live.

Jean C. Summey
resides in
Rock Hill, South Carolina.

It's a Wrap!

Make your own wrapping paper. Rubber stamping on brown packing paper, plain white wrapping paper, or even brown paper grocery bags can be an economical way to wrap your gifts. It is a lot of fun to design your own paper and it makes your gifts seem more personal. Children also love to design and stamp their own paper. Matching gift cards are easily made by folding an index card in half. Rubber stamps can also be used to make your own Christmas cards, or just to brighten up the envelopes of your store-bought cards!

Linda Slaughter
resides in
Park Ridge, Illinois.

A LASTING LEGACY

Perhaps you have grandchildren who receive far too many material items at Christmas. Why not purchase a savings bond, or silver coins that could have some value for them in the future! Coin packets, purchased for each year of their life, could be one legacy you leave for them.

Joyce Friesner
resides in
Ligonier, Indiana.

CHRISTMAS PUPPETS

Our children are at the ages now when they love to put on puppet shows. Shortly before Christmas we tell them the Christmas story in installments and they then make puppets of the characters that were in the story that day. (Any type of puppet will do.) We do this until the story and all the puppets have been completed. Then on Christmas Eve they put on their own performance, from the angel visiting Mary to the family fleeing to Egypt. (Painting or coloring scenery is optional but it adds a lot to the show!)

Christine Beckett
resides in
Matawan, New Jersey.

REMEMBER

VERSATILE BASKETS

Gift baskets make great gifts. You can make your own baskets or buy plain ones and decorate them with ribbons and lace. Place fabric, a towel, or a doily inside as a lining. Customize the basket according to the receiver's personality, likes and dislikes, and so on. Here are some ideas: fishing tackle, soaps, perfumes, cards and travel games, CDs or cassettes, jewelry, miniatures or collectibles, books, stationery, candy, jam, bathtub toys, doll clothes, tools, sewing things, socks, and so on. Be creative!

Loretta Arts
resides in
Valdez, Alaska.

CHRISTMAS MEMORY ALBUM

Our family's Christmas memories have been put together in a family Christmas album. Inside are photographs, descriptions of our celebrations, current world events, and many thoughts of the holiday. I look forward to the day when my children are grown and they too can treasure the album.

Annette McEndarfer
resides in
Worcester, Massachusetts.

Last year my sister and I invited my mother and her four sisters to my house to make these ornaments. It was a wonderful reason to get together and have lunch and "just talk."

1 cup applesauce
¾ cup cinnamon
2 tablespoons ground cloves
2 tablespoons nutmeg
2 tablespoons ginger

Mix all ingredients together. Roll onto wax paper until ⅛-inch thick. Cut out with cookie cutters. Poke hole with a drinking straw to hang. Put on wire rack and dry three days, turning daily.

Since they have to dry in one place friends and relatives have another reason to "have to get together again" to claim the ornaments.

P.S. Another good idea might be to make these ornaments on Thanksgiving and use them as favors when you get together again for Christmas.

> *Linda J. Beck*
> *resides in*
> *Chicora, Pennsylvania.*

REMEMBER

One shake enlivens salads, meat, poultry, and vegetables! To make, mix together the following herbs:

2 teaspoons garlic powder
2 teaspoons onion powder
2 teaspoons paprika
2 teaspoons white pepper
2 teaspoons dry mustard
1 teaspoon powdered thyme
1 teaspoon ground celery seed

I buy antique salt shakers at garage sales or flea markets and fill with herb shaker recipe to give as gifts.

June Blackford
resides in
Nicholasville, Kentucky.

A CHILD'S VERY OWN TREE

You will need a little pine tree or branch about four or five inches tall, a plant pot, some dirt, popcorn, and anything else you wish for decorations.

Take the pot and fill it with dirt and plant the tree in the pot. Take the popcorn and put it on the pine needles. Then put it in your room. You will have your very own Christmas tree!

Alicia Del Vescova
resides in
Round Top, New York.

The Family Treasury of Great Holiday Ideas

I became a single father when my daughter was three and my son was one. Changing houses, starting day care, and trying to rebuild a new life was a challenge to tradition and routine. Christmas found us in the habit of reading a Bible chapter every night during our snack, right before bed. I decided to introduce the Advent wreath tradition into our readings, making sure that we started and finished the Christmas story between Thanksgiving and December 25th.

After picking out our reusable wreath, I placed the manger figures of Mary, Joseph, and Jesus in the center, snuggled into Colorado evergreens. Then, I put the crèche with the animal figures toward the bottom and into the greenery of the Christmas tree, about child-eye level.

We know when Christmas has arrived because Old St. Nick not only finishes his cookies and milk, he also places Mary, Joseph, and the baby Jesus into the crèche, announcing the birth and highlighting the real meaning of Christmas.

Through the years we have collected a series of angels to hover around the crèche, making it an eye catcher to all who see the tree. By Christmas Eve, my now ten- and thirteen-year-old children have found the ornaments that look like tiny wrapped packages and have placed those near the base of the crèche as presents for the new baby. I look forward, as a grandpa someday, to seeing this tradition repeated in two other homes.

Patrick, John, and Lauren Batchelder
reside in
Boulder, Colorado.

REMEMBER

At Christmas we especially think of loved ones no longer with us. To remember, with joy instead of sadness, is sometimes difficult. I chose to make a remembrance ornament for my son Monte using a picture of him sitting at a Christmas tree that was a happy memory. It is meaningful to me, a small remembrance, made with great love. The spirit of Christmas is giving with love, and remembering with love.

Frances Moss Taylor
resides in
Danville, Virginia.

Keep Winter Bright

After Christmas is over, I put the greeting cards I received in an attractive basket next to the phone and use them for notes. Each time I make a note I reread and enjoy the holiday message once again and remember happy times with the friend or relative who sent the card to me. One of the best things about Christmas is being in touch with dear ones. In this way, Christmas brightens all the winter months.

Mary Louise Colln
is a writer of inspirational romance and also
works as a registered nurse. She resides in
Joplin, Missouri.

CHRISTMAS CARDS PLUS

Each fall we have our family picture taken at a place that offers mini-portrait packages. We then enclose in Christmas cards our picture, a newsletter (a summary of the past year written by each family member), and a Gospel tract. It is a good opportunity to show God's love toward others and to witness of His presence in our lives during the past year.

GIFTS FOR GRANDMOTHERS

For years I faced the dilemma of what to give my grandmothers for Christmas. They did not need or want ornamental objects or "things." So I tried something different a few years ago: I put together a decorated box filled with delightful items. Small cans of fruits or vegetables, puddings, crackers, cheese, jellies, notepaper, snack foods, bath oil, and so on have been included. My grandmothers look forward to these packages every year.

Susan Colwell
resides in
Windsor, New York.

CHRISTMAS CARD TREE

One year we had just moved in and were unable to unpack our Christmas tree decorations. As Christmas cards arrived at our home, we would punch a hole in the corner of each one, slip a ribbon through the hole, and tie the card to the Christmas tree. You could still read the cards and the tree looked so pretty!

Nancy Price
resides in
Brooksville, Florida.

REMEMBER

Let the children decorate a basket. Fill the basket with goodies that an elderly friend could use:

- Canned food
- Fruit
- Nuts
- Stationery
- Stamps
- Assorted cards (birthday, get well)

Take the basket to an elderly friend or neighbor. Put the basket on the doorknob or by the door. Ring the door bell and hide!*

CREATE YOUR OWN NATIVITY SCENE

Each Christmas we pull out a very special nativity scene. It would win no art contest. The little play dough figures look the worse for wear. One angel has a broken wing and her halo is lost. The camel only has three toothpick legs. The wise men have long ago lost their gifts. But it still gets center stage at our house. Why? Because it is one of our most special holiday memories and traditions.

It all started one holiday season years ago when the three boys were bored and hyper. We were temporarily living in the U.S., and our Christmas decorations, including our nativity scene, were packed away at our home in Austria. With more time than money or talent, we decided to create our own nativity scene.

Using the Creative Clay recipe tat follows, we molded our little people. They somewhat resembled little Fisher Price people, just a little more (or perhaps a lot more) rustic! We let them dry and them painted each with tempera paints. The following Saturday we took a walk through the woods and picked up anything of interest, such as moss, roots, acorns, sticks, stones, and pine cones. We brought our "treasures" home, and on a piece of plywood, we constructed our very own nativity scene. The manger was crafted from a root covered with moss. Pine cones served as trees. The final touch was adding our little nativity people and animals that we had made

---

*Used by permission of Thomas Nelson, Inc., Publishers.

The Family Treasury of Great Holiday Ideas

from the play dough. When we returned to our home in Austria, we took our little people along. Each year we took a family walk in the woods picking up goodies, and later at home we reconstructed our manger scene. How special it has been each Christmas to bring out our little homemade nativity people—broken wings, broken legs, and all. They bring back great memories of Christmases past.

So when boredom threatens to strike at your home, pull out the play dough recipe. Make your own nativity people, take your own walk in the woods, assemble your own simple nativity scene, and add to your family's special Christmas memories.

CREATIVE CLAY:

- 1 cup cornstarch
- 2 cups baking soda (1-pound package)
- 1¼ cups cold water

Stir the cornstarch and baking soda together. Mix in cold water and stir over medium heat until the mixture has the consistency of mashed potatoes. Turn onto a plate and cover with a damp cloth until cool enough to handle. Then knead. Use immediately or store in an airtight container.*

(Turn the page for another tradition submitted by Dave and Claudia Arp.)

———————

*Used by permission of Thomas Nelson, Inc., Publishers.

REMEMBER

Do you want to send a very unique and unusual Christmas present to a family you love? Let us tell you about a memory-building gift we received from our dear friends, the Peddicords. They sent us "The Twelve Days of Christmas." As we opened the Christmas box, the first thing we saw was a book of Christmas carols with this note:

> SING THE SONG ON PAGE 26 BEFORE OPENING THIS PRESENT OR SHARING IT WITH OTHERS. SIT TOGETHER AND HAVE TIME WITHOUT OTHER DISTRACTIONS TOO, IF POSSIBLE. WE'RE THINKING OF YOU THIS CHRISTMAS! LOVE, CLARK AND ANN

You guessed it! The song was "The Twelve Days of Christmas," and in the box were twelve gifts to be opened. Each was numbered so we knew how to proceed, and each represented one of the twelve days of Christmas. Why not have some fun this year and send "The Twelve Days of Christmas" to a family you know. Use your imagination. Here are some suggestions to get you started.

- **Day 1**—a partridge in a pear tree—This could be "homemade art" drawn by one of the children.
- **Day 2**—two turtle doves—Our friends sent a small framed picture of two birds that is still on our memento shelf.
- **Day 3**—three French hens—Make three chicken Christmas tree ornaments out of felt.
- **Day 4**—four calling birds—Draw a picture of four birds all talking on the telephone.
- **Day 5**—five golden rings—Make five gold napkin rings out of felt. Simply cut in strips (2 inches by 6 inches) and sew the short ends together.
- **Day 6**—six geese a-laying—What about six chocolate eggs?

We've gotten you started. On the last six, you're on your own.

- **Day 7**—seven swans a-swimming—
- **Day 8**—eight maids a-milking—
- **Day 9**—nine ladies dancing—

The Family Treasury of Great Holiday Ideas

- **Day 10**—ten lords a-leaping—
- **Day 11**—eleven pipers piping—
- **Day 12**—twelve drummers drumming—

Wrap the gifts individually, label them, and send this unique gift on its way. Be sure to include a copy of the song, "The Twelve Days of Christmas," and a note suggesting that they set aside at least thirty minutes to an hour to open and enjoy your gift. Then sit back and wait for their happy response!*

Dave and Claudia Arp
are the founders of Marriage Alive
International, a worldwide ministry.
Currently they write a column for Christian
Parenting Today *magazine and host a two-*
minute radio program,
"The Family Workshop."

*Used by permission of Thomas Nelson, Inc., Publishers.

AN EASY ADVENT CALENDAR

My two-year-old daughter and I made our own Advent calendar last year and it didn't cost us anything. Take a large piece of cardboard and paint a large evergreen tree, almost to the edges of cardboard. Punch two holes in the top of the cardboard with a paper punch and tie a red ribbon through holes to hang it on the wall. We then sorted through old Christmas cards and cut out small pictures. Christmas dolls, candles, snowflakes, sleighs, bells, angels, stars, candy canes, and so on are some examples. Put these in an envelope. Each day, starting on 1 December, Rachel and I would get out the envelope and spread out several cut-out pictures. Rachel would pick out one and we would then glue it on the tree wherever she wanted. She loved doing the Advent calendar and always reminded me before breakfast each day.

Mary Jane Allio
resides in
Tionesta, Pennsylvania.

REMEMBER

The year our first child was two years old, I let her help me decorate the family Christmas tree. When we finished, I had a small two-foot artificial tree I had purchased with nonbreakable decorations, most of them homemade. She and I put "her" tree up and then I explained that she could not touch the big tree because it was just to look at, but she could touch her tree and do what she wanted with it.

That evening her daddy came home and she grabbed his hand to take him in to view the trees. Pointing to the family tree, she said, "Don't touch it, Daddy." Then she pointed to her tree and said, "That's the Touch-It Tree."

From that holiday on, until our family had grown and moved away to college, we had a Touch-It Tree. The decorations changed as our children grew older but it was always their tree to put up and do with as they wished. As little children they often dragged it around the house, putting it up and taking it down many times during December, but they never touched the big tree and never broke an ornament on the big tree. When they were old enough they made their own ornaments, and one year all of the ornaments were edible. This is a tradition that will be carried on in their families when they have children because it was so special for them.

Judy Lovitt
resides in Ogden, Utah.

GRANDMA'S ORNAMENTS

Christmas celebrations always bring to mind a rush of memories. Each memory is as individual as the year it was created, and all are cherished reminders of days gone by.

Some years ago my mother struck upon an idea for making each year a special celebration for her grandchildren. She purchases for each one a personalized, dated tree ornament. Sometimes the ornaments represent the child's interest or hobby and sometimes they are all alike, representing something special to the giver.

The children always look forward to "Grandma's ornaments" and it's every bit as much fun for my mother.

When it comes time to decorate the Christmas tree, we make a special event of it with eggnog and goodies. We pull out dusty boxes of Christmas decorations and as we sort through the ornaments the memories come to life. "I remember when . . ." is probably the most often-heard phrase of the day.

While we join together to celebrate the birth of our Lord, we celebrate not only the family He's blessed us with but the memories of our lives together. I believe it's the love we have through Him for one another, as well as the good and bad times we've shared, that makes us a family.

When our children grow up and leave home, I want them to take not only "Grandma's ornaments," but eighteen or more years of memories of celebrating a family Christmas.

Tracie J. Peterson
is a regular columnist for a Christian
newspaper as well as a writer of inspirational
romances (under the pen name, Janelle
Jamison). She resides in Topeka, Kansas.

AN ORNAMENTAL CENTERPIECE

Make a pretty decoration by filling a clear glass bowl with glass Christmas ornaments and a string of either colored or clear tiny lights. Add a few sprigs of green on top to complete a delightful decoration for a cupboard or centerpiece (use battery operated lights).

Here's a variation of that idea. Before the Christmas dinner have a glass ornament on each plate with an empty glass bowl in the center of the table. Each person around the table then tells one thing that he or she is thankful for and places the ornament in the bowl.

Kathy Offord
resides in Barron, Wisconsin.

REMEMBER

Small packages are placed on the plates at the beginning of our Christmas dinner. These gifts are chosen with the intention of bringing our minds back to Christ after a busy season of excitement, shopping, and gift giving.

Among our favorite gifts have been small heart paper clips that told of Jesus' love, name-bearing bookmarks with Scriptures for each person, and polished rocks in small Christmas stockings. Along with the rock each person got a Scripture telling how Christ is our Rock. After reading the Scriptures aloud each person was encouraged to keep his rock in a pocket or coin purse as a reminder that we can rely on the Lord.

Sylvia Stone
resides in
Medical Lake, Washington.

THE FAMILY TREE

When my children finished high school and college, I cross-stitched graduation caps with names, dates, and schools and made ornaments for the tree. I also made ornaments from pictures of the children in Santa's lap and of grandparents who are no longer with us as a good memory of Christmases past. Now my grandson will learn of his family tree from our Christmas tree.

Mildred S. Barton
resides in
Anderson, South Carolina.

The Family Treasury of Great Holiday Ideas

When times were tough and money was scarce, we began a tradition that each family member still looks forward to every Christmas.

For each family member with a stocking hanging at the fireplace, prepare one personal promise. A simple pledge to perform some duty can be scratched on a 3 x 5 card and inserted by the promisor, who signs his or her name at the bottom. Promises can be used like certificates, redeemable during the new year, by simply pulling out the "coupon" and collecting on the promise.

Promises may be for attitude changes, chores, special occasions, just use your imagination! Some samples of promises might include the following:

> One foot rub
> I'll do your kitchen duty
> One movie night, popcorn and all
> I will clean up my room, no arguments
> I promise to be more thankful
> Date night: You choose the spot
> I'll wash the dog (or the car, and so on)
> I'll make lunches in the morning
> I give you the day off:
>   no housework, no homework—relaxation of your
>   choice
> Read a book with you (for a little one)
> One free manicure

These very personal gift certificates are a special way of saying you care. (The trick is to keep them where you can find them again!) It's always a special moment when, in emptying the stockings, we all share our promises, and revel in the thought we can redeem the coupon in a desperate time of need!

SURPRISE CALENDAR

A special gift Grandma or Grandpa would cherish from their grandchildren, or grandparents can prepare for parents of small

REMEMBER

193

children. The calendar picture for each month is personalize
for the recipient!

During the year plan to get together with family member
and ask each one to draw a picture that represents a calend
month. They may be scribbled in crayon, smeared in wate
color, scratched in pencil, or more professionally rendered b
an older family member. Just be sure all twelve pictures are o
the same size paper (8½ x 11 inches or larger) and each on
represents a particular month. A special family occasion coul
even be pictured: a wedding anniversary, birthday, graduatio
and so on. Here are some other suggestions:

January	Snowpeople, winter clothes
February	Presidents' birthdays, valentines
March	Wind, spring flowers breaking through
April	Easter events, lilies, church
May	Maypole, Memorial Day, Mother's Day
June	Father's Day, graduation
July	American flags, summer fun
August	Hot summer days, out-of-school activities
September	Back to school, Labor Day
October	Fall leaves, colors
November	Thanksgiving turkey, Indians, pilgrims
December	Christmas memories and fun

After October the new year's calendars are available. Pu
chase any one in which your pictures will fit (if the pictur
space is larger, just paste up on construction paper bac
ground). Glue your personalized pictures over the printed one
and wrap up for a special Christmas gift. The children wh
helped create the calendar will be excited because most likel
they've long forgotten the picture they drew. What a splendi
way to remind a special someone they are loved, every mont
of the year!

Lee Ezell
*is a well-known author and speaker on
women's issues. Among her books are* The
Cinderella Syndrome *(Bantam Books, Inc.)
and* The Missing Piece *(Servant).*

The Family Treasury of Great Holiday Ideas

s our Christmas cards arrive, my little girl opens them and ᴛen we read and tape them on the door. After New Year's Day go through and cut them on the folded edge. The sides with ᴛe picture I save. Some are appropriate to use to write on the ᴀck and send in an envelope as thank yous for Christmas gifts. ᴑthers are usable as Christmas postcards for next year or for ᴀrious craft projects. Finally, some I send to St. Jude's Ranch ᴑr Children where the fronts of cards are recycled (100 St. ᴀde's Street, Boulder City, NV 89005).

Mary Jane Allio
resides in
Tionesta, Pennsylvania.

ᴀDVENT PRAYER CHAIN

ᴴere's an idea for a Sunday school class, large extended family, ᴛ neighborhood. Make an Advent prayer chain for each house-ᴑld, writing prayer concerns on colored strips of construction ᴀper. Class members or family or friends write the same con-ᴇrn on twenty-eight (or fewer) pieces of paper so that each ᴇight prayers are being raised for specific concerns. Join the ᴴains together and rejoice in being faithful in prayer for some-ᴛe you care about.

Andy Caughey
resides in
Harrington Park, New Jersey.

REMEMBER

On the first day of December we put up a "Jesus Tree." The tree is made of green felt and is placed on the refrigerator with magnets. Each night our two sons tape ornaments also made of felt on the tree. They choose one type of ornament to place on the tree and continue each night until all ornaments are on the tree. We have made about twenty of each ornament and each type has its own significance. The ornaments include the following:

mangers	to show how Jesus was born
crosses	to show how Jesus died
blood drops	to show He shed His blood for us
candlesticks	to signify Jesus is the Light of the World
stars	He is the bright and morning star (also the star led the wise men)
Bibles	God's Holy Word and Jesus is the Word
lambs	Jesus is the Lamb of God
bread	Jesus is the Bread of Life

Because the tree is quite visible and different, visitors to our home ask about it. We explain the ornaments, enabling us to witness to our friends. The Jesus Tree is our way of keeping Christ in Christmas.

The Mike Hill Family
resides in
Ripley, Mississippi.

Although we put our tree up the first part of December, we stack all presents by the piano. Under the tree we place all the presents that Jesus gives to us.

We take wooden blocks of assorted sizes (scraps from 2 x 4, 2 x 6, and 2 x 12 lumber) and cover them with white butcher paper (wrap like presents). Each day we take one and write on the outside something that Jesus gives us (forgiveness, inner peace, strength, and so on). We rotate days so a different family member gets to name a present at least once a week.

When Christmas arrives we have a thank-you prayer, thanking the Lord for all the presents He has given us. Our tree is overflowing with presents and our hearts are overflowing with thankfulness.

A THANK-YOU BOX

This is a special heartfelt present for you to give to Jesus. Take and cover a shoebox with wrapping paper. Cover the lid separately so you can open it without unwrapping.

On a piece of paper write a thank-you note to Jesus for something specific He has done for you. Fill the box with thank-you notes and read them occasionally during the season when things get hectic. Keep it handy all year long and fill it with thank yous. By next Christmas you'll need a bigger box!

Diane Armstrong
resides in
Sedro-Woolley, Washington.

REMEMBER

For several years we have had a Christmas "Sweetswap" at our church where six to eight couples exchange Christmas ornaments and cookies. The twist to it is that each *wife* handmakes the ornaments and each *husband* makes the cookies from scratch, each *with absolutely no help from the other!* If there are eight couples involved, each wife is responsible for providing seven handmade ornaments and each husband is to provide seven dozen homemade cookies.

We meet in a home after Sunday evening service about two weeks prior to Christmas. Each couple brings a covered dish to share along with their exchange items. After snacking and socializing, the ornaments and dozens of cookies are exchanged usually in little decorative sacks or plates with the ornament attached. The husband shares any bits of wisdom or humor he encountered as he made his cookies, and those listening offer their comments concerning the appearance of his delicacies.

Everyone looks forward to this very fun evening. There is a lot of "ribbing" and good clean Christian fun shared during the evening.

As a plus, we now ask that each couple bring an extra dozen cookies and an ornament and we invite the minister and his wife to come and enjoy the fun. Their ticket in, rather than come empty-handed, is to bring a covered dish to share.

Marilyn Pfeifer
resides in
Washington C.H., Ohio.

The Family Treasury of Great Holiday Ideas

These French paper lanterns, called *lampions*, can be made by youngsters to make your entry say "welcome." Make your own luminaria bags from sturdy glossy paper or from simple brown paper lunch bags. In either case, fold and make cut-outs in the bag to let light show through. You may glue colored tissue paper inside to diffuse the light and give a stained-glass effect, or you can leave the bag as it is. For each bag you'll need a glass jar. Put some sand in the bottom of the jar and a votive candle on top of the sand. Luminarias should last for many holiday nights.*

CHRISTMAS LONG AGO

Grandparents can make very special cards for their grandchildren by sharing what Christmas was like in their youth. Type or write these memories and then glue them onto colored paper folders. Make a different one for each child in the family.*

*From 101 IDEAS FOR THE BEST-EVER CHRISTMAS.
Copyright © 1992 by Caryl Waller Krueger.
Excerpted by permission of the publisher, Abingdon Press.

MEMORY CANDLES

Almost forty years ago when we were living in the Belgian Congo (now Zaire) the idea came to me to save memories by melting the remnants of birthday and Christmas candles and making one candle to represent the whole year. That first candle wasn't very large. A small fruit juice can was more than adequate to hold the melted wax from three sets of birthday candles, my husband's, our daughter's, and mine, and the few stubs of red and green Christmas candles that we didn't save for the next year. When it was unmolded it stood about three inches high.

As years passed we added three more birthdays and each

REMEMBER

one yielded more candles. When we returned to the United States to live, I was quicker to discard used candles. There were other festive occasions, like wedding anniversaries, graduations, and prom parties, which provided candles, so my memory candles grew bigger.

Each year thereafter we brought out our memory candles early in December and arranged them on the piano. Christmas Eve we lighted them and enjoyed their glow while we sang carols and read the Christmas story.

When it was time to leave our home and move into a retirement complex, I stopped making candles. I considered remelting all the candles and making just one big one but my daughters didn't like that idea.

They picked out the ones with special memories for them—wedding year, graduation, first baby's birthday—and then they divided the others. Today the candles are set out in their homes, and one daughter has continued the tradition of making her own candle each year.

When I picture all those candles lighted and the family sitting around them singing "Joy to the World," the memories return, just as precious as when I first melted a few wax remnants and poured them into a glass.

Margaret S. Jump
resides in
Lewisburg, Pennsylvania.

And Mary arose in those days, and went into the hill country with haste, into a city of Juda; and entered into the house of Zacharias, and saluted Elisabeth.

(Luke 1:39-40, KJV)

COOKIE CUTTER FRAMES

Preserve Christmas memories and build an ornament collection at the same time! Select your favorite cutter shape as well as a cherished photo of your child from that year. Simply trim the photo to size and glue the edges to the cookie cutter. Decorate with ribbon, paint, and glitter as desired. Remember to date the back of the photo for an accurate recording of your child's growing-up years.

MORE STOCKINGS

One of my favorite funny but practical gifts to give is a fluffy red Christmas stocking stuffed with . . . what else? Stockings!

Janet LaSpina
resides in
Dunmore, Pennsylvania.

A GALLERY OF GREETINGS

Each year we select the greeting card we like best from those received and frame it. We date the framed card and include the address and name of the sender in order to identify later on. Through the years we have accumulated quite a gallery of Christmas scenes. These framed cards are displayed along with our other holiday decorations each year.

Valeria Richard
resides in
Escatawpa, Mississippi.

REMEMBER

1 cup instant tea mix
1 box peach gelatin
2 cups granulated sugar

Combine all ingredients in a large bowl; mix well. Store in an airtight container. To serve, stir about 2 teaspoons tea mix into 8 ounces hot water.

If given as a gift, put the mixture into an airtight plastic bag and make a fabric bag as a covering.

To make a fabric bag, cut a 7- x 23-inch piece of fabric. With right sides together, sew sides of bag together. Turn bag right side out, turn top edge of bag under ¼ inch and topstitch. Tie two 18-inch pieces of ribbon in a bow around the bag. For a more festive touch, tuck a sprig of holly under the bow. Include inside a card with serving instructions.

*Sharyn Bischof
resides in
Bridgeview, Illinois.*

And it came to pass, that, when Elisabeth heard the salutation of Mary, the babe leaped in her womb; and Elisabeth was filled with the Holy Ghost: And she spake out with a loud voice, and said, Blessed art thou among women, and blessed is the fruit of thy womb.

(Luke 1:41-42, KJV)

POTPOURRI BAG TREE ORNAMENTS

1 small rubber band
4 x 6 inches fancy lace
10 inches of ¼-inch ribbon, color coordinated with lace
½ cup potpourri

Take 4 x 6-inch piece of fancy lace for each bag. With right sides together, sew sides of bag, leaving top and bottom sides open. Turn right side out and stitch across bottom above fancy border so it is free flowing. Fill with potpourri of your choice. Take the ribbon and weave it in and out around the top. Take the small rubber band and wrap it around the top to keep potpourri in the bag. Pull ribbon tight so it looks like a small handbag. Hang it on your tree! (When you take down your tree, store potpourri in an airtight plastic bag. Potpourri bags can be refreshed yearly as needed.)

Rhonda Gwara
resides in
Rome, New York.

WISHBONE ORNAMENTS

My mother seemed to always find ways to add to our family fun. At Thanksgiving she would set aside the turkey's wishbone, wash it, and let it dry. Then she would show us children how to wrap it with aluminum foil. When it was time to trim our Christmas tree, we looped thread or a thin ribbon to the top of the wishbone, and hung it on our tree. As the years went by, we added more and more glistening wishbones to our lucky-looking Christmas trees.

Charlotte Adelsperger
resides in
Overland Park, Kansas.

REMEMBER

The first Christmas after our marriage my husband and I spent several hours searching for the perfect little cedar tree to place on our dining room table. Its little branches would not hold many ornaments, but among them was a beautiful little charm with the date engraved on it from my parents. Each year Mother would search carefully for just the right charm to add to our collection. Sometimes the charms depicted a symbol of Christmas, such as the Holy Family, or a special event, such as the bicentennial year. One special charm was a tiny silver-framed picture of our daughter Jennifer dressed as Mrs. Santa in her kindergarten graduation play. Each year as we take them out of their tiny jewelry boxes we are delighted to refresh our memories through Mother and Daddy's thoughtfulness.

Mickey and William Harris
reside in
Escatawpa, Mississippi.

Therefore the Lord himself shall give you a sign; Behold, a virgin shall conceive, and bear a son, and shall call his name Immanuel.

(Isaiah 7:14, KJV)

The Family Treasury of Great Holiday Ideas

A few years ago my husband took the trunk of a cedar tree, cut off all the branches, and drilled twenty-five candle-sized holes in it. We then put it in a plastic bag in our freezer for two weeks to kill any bugs. Each December first we place one white candle in the middle hole and twenty-four red candles in the other holes. I place fake holly around it and set it up on our fireplace hearth. The first day of December we light one end candle, read a special story, pray, and sing a song, then blow out the candle. The second day of December we light the candles on each end of the log and have our devotion. Each day of December we light one more candle than we did the night before. By Christmas, the twenty-fifth white candle in the middle is also lit. The Advent log makes a beautiful decoration and helps us slow down the busyness of the season: no party or activity is allowed to steal our candle-devotion time. Our family is able to quiet down and remember the real meaning of Christmas.

Kimberly Miller Wentworth
resides in
Colbert, Georgia.

And she brought forth her firstborn son, and wrapped him in swaddling clothes, and laid him in a manger; because there was no room for them in the inn.

(Luke 2:7, KJV)

REMEMBER

How to Keep Holidays Stressless

1. **Ask your family members to share their favorite holiday** memory. You may be surprised how few meals and toys they mention. We did this at our church Christmas party one year and, to my surprise, very few of them recall special holiday memories. If this be the case, create some memories. Make your time count—a memory lasts forever, but toys get broken.

2. **Try not to do everything yourself.** Small children can help, just lower your perfection a little and allow those small hands to bake and decorate. These experiences may stay in their memories long after the holidays are over. Even if your husband is unable to help you the rest of the year, the Christmas spirit will inspire him. Ask him to help you or ask if he could run some errands near where he works.

3. Settle family matters ahead of the holiday time. Families are often separated by divorce or geographic distance and disputes can arise. Try to make all the arrangements well ahead of time. If you have out of town guests, decide where they will stay and let them know before they arrive if they really need to be at a motel. Share your time equally and fairly with each set of grandparents or take turns from year to year. Avoid overcommitment—it can make for situations where people are overtired and overreact.

4. Don't gain weight. Feeling fat in party clothes can really add to your stress and tension. Overeating can make you feel absolutely awful. Try to schedule the same exercise you normally do. If you are not exercising now make it a goal for the new year.

   There will be a great deal of extra goodies around, but be selective about what you eat. Stick to the things that are worth it, like your favorites that you see only at holiday time.

   Place yourself next to the food table where the fruit or veggie platter is. If you decide now not to overdo it, you won't have to make that New Year resolution to lose weight later.

5. Remember what really matters. As Christians, Christmas is the time for celebrating the birth of Christ and everything else comes after that special celebration. The hassles will take

The Family Treasury of Great Holiday Ideas

care of themselves.

6. Watch your finances carefully. Talk about tension and depression! Overspending will do it especially if you've overcharged and have those bills to look forward to later. Ask the Lord to help you in this area so you won't get caught up in the spirit of things and buy much more than you budgeted for.

   Remember that a handmade gift or baked item can be more valuable than an expensive one. Special phone calls or a coupon for an "after Christmas lunch treat" can mean as much to a friend as an expensive gift they may not use or like. Set your budget and stick to it. Many people have a special Christmas fund set aside. That makes it easy and when that's gone, it's gone. Otherwise, spread your purchases over a period of time and charge only the amount you intend to spend. That's why we suggest you begin your gift shopping early in November so it doesn't all come at once.

7. It's okay to say no. You'd like to do it all, be everywhere, and see everything. But for today's busy woman, it just can't be. Don't be afraid to say, "No, we need this time together as a family" or "No, I can't bake the extra cookies but I'd be happy to buy some." Don't feel guilty about those things you simply can't do.

8. Plan some time for yourself. You can read a book, listen to a tape or music, take a bubble bath with a candle lit, get a good haircut, have your nails polished, or maybe even buy yourself a new nightgown, blouse, or holiday sweater. By taking care of yourself, that last-minute hassle about your appearance won't happen.

9. Christmas will come regardless if you've done everything on your lists or not. Do those things which really matter and let the others fall where they may.

   Family, friends, and above all the true meaning of Christmas is what counts. Remember 60 percent of our stress is caused by disorganization.*

Emilie Barnes
is a noted speaker, seminar leader, and author.
More Hours in My Day *and* The Spirit of
Loveliness *(Harvest House Publishers) are*
among her best-known books.

*Excerpt from: THE COMPLETE HOLIDAY ORGANIZER by Emilie Barnes.
Copyright © 1987 by Harvest House Publishers, Eugene, Oregon 97402.
Used by permission.

REMEMBER

We have been painfully aware in recent years that two specia
people are now absent from the family circle, Jim's father an
my uncle. . . . I am reminded at this moment of a praye
expressed by Jim's father during the final year of his life. . . .

He said, "Lord, we have enjoyed being together so much thi
past week, and you have been good to make this time possible
But Lord, we are realistic enough to know that life moves or
and that circumstances will not always be as we enjoy ther
today. We understand that a day is coming when the fellowshi
we now share will be but a memory to those who remain. That'
why I want to thank you for bringing love into our lives for thi
season, and for the happiness we have experienced with on
another."

. . . Circumstances will inevitably change; nothing in this lif
is eternal or permanent. But while God grants us breath, w
will enjoy one another to the fullest and spread our love as fa
and wide as possible.

Thanksgiving at the Dobson home is an occasion for th
celebration of that philosophy.*

Shirley Dobson
is the chairman of the National Day of Prayer
and serves on the Board of Directors of the
Focus on the Family Ministry. She is married
to psychologist and best-selling author
Dr. James C. Dobson.

Let's Make a Memory, Gloria Gaither and Shirley Dobson,
Copyright © 1983, Word, Inc., Dallas, Texas. Used by permission.

Thanksgiving Day is set aside each year for the specific purpose of thanking God for all of our many blessings.

In my book *Passport to Heaven*, are two verses from God's Word instructing us to give thanks.

"Giving thanks always for all things unto God and the Father in the name of our Lord Jesus Christ."   (Ephesians 5:20)

"In every thing give thanks: for this is the will of God in Christ Jesus concerning you."   (1 Thessalonians 5:18)

Of course there are many more verses in the Bible encouraging us to thank God for all things.

Mildred Purrett
resides in
Lyons, Colorado.

THE TWELVE SURPRISES OF CHRISTMAS

As a take-off of this theme, my young son chooses twelve people whom he feels should receive special gifts during the twelve days leading up to Christmas. These gifts are often handmade and are not given in the spirit that something will be received in return. Sometimes we choose a person we don't know, maybe living in a nursing home, to be the recipient of such a gift. The real joy in this is the lesson of sharing that it teaches all of us.

Nancy Price
resides in
Brooksville, Florida.

REMEMBER

Christians know Advent, a word which means "coming," as a time of preparation and reflection. For the course of four Sundays preceding Christmas Eve, a period of twenty-two to twenty-eight days, we anticipate celebrating the birth of Christ.

Scripture readings for Advent center around the prophecy of a Messiah and His birth in Bethlehem. They tell, too, of our life together in His name, and of His promise to return as reigning King and judge of the world.

Advent is like a light in the darkness. For us it will always be a time of great hope. A King called Immanuel has come into our midst, and "He will save His people from their sins."

The Advent wreath represents God's never-ending love and eternity, and the surrounding evergreens, the four Sundays. Set among the evergreens are the four candles of Advent: the first, the Candle of Light; the second, the Candle of Hope; the third, the Candle of Joy; and on the fourth Sunday the Candle of Love is lit. A fifth candle in the center of the wreath, called the Christ Candle, is lit on Christmas Eve or Christmas Day to represent the bright light of the Messiah, Jesus, who declared, "I am the Light of the world."

Fred A. Hartley
serves as pastor at the Lilburn Alliance
Church, Lilburn, Georgia. He is also a popular
author, as demonstrated by
The Teenage Book of Manners . . . PLEASE!
(Barbour Books).

The Spirit of Giving

A few years ago while planning a Christmas party with my junior high girls' Sunday school class, the students asked if they could exchange gifts, something I'd discouraged in past years. Some of my students lived in the inner city and came on the church buses; I knew that any extra expense around Christmas

The Family Treasury of Great Holiday Ideas

would be a burden to their families.

However, I didn't want to squelch the spirit of giving, and I remembered what great fun it was to exchange gifts at school or Sunday school as a child. "All right," I finally said. "But here are the rules. You may not spend more than one dollar on the gift that you bring."

"A dollar!" cried several girls in unison, as if they'd practiced it. "What can you buy for that?" wailed another. I wondered, then, if perhaps my idea hadn't been so good, but I wasn't about to back down. After all, it's the thought that should be important when giving or getting a gift, not how much was spent— and setting such a strict limit would insure that the girls gave some thought to their gifts.

"It can be something you buy, or make," I told them, hoping that my show of enthusiasm would be contagious. "And at the party, we'll display the gifts you brought after they're opened. Just don't cheat—keep the price under a dollar."

There were no more protests, and I knew I had them when a girl raised her hand and asked, "Does that include tax?"

"You may go over a dollar to pay sales tax. Any questions?" There were no questions, so in my best imitation of a football coach I said, "I want to see some creativity, whether you buy or make the gift. Class dismissed."

Three weeks later our party was held in the fellowship hall of the church. I was anxious to see how the girls had done with their assignment. After we drew names and swapped gifts, each student, one at a time, stood and displayed what she'd been given. And how clever the girls had been! One of the gifts was a simple cardboard earring box, covered with velvet, lace, and fake pearls. A couple of girls had made fancy hair ribbons. Store-bought gifts included a diary, lip gloss, and fun things like bubble bath.

Best of all was how much the class enjoyed it. "Can we do it again next year?" several girls asked me. "You bet!" was my reply.

Kate Blackwell
is a popular writer of inspirational romance
who resides in Baton Rouge, Louisiana.
Among her recent books is Shores of Promise
(Heartsong Presents).

REMEMBER

My family decided to broaden our gift giving by sharing with those with greater physical needs. We set aside a designated amount of money and purchased gifts for the families of prisoners through Project Angel Tree®. Our daughter helped pick out toys, clothes, books, candy, and more. We all wrapped the gifts and included in each a tract and a telephone number if there are questions. The gifts are then delivered to families by Project Angel Tree® workers.*

Jan DePasqualin
resides in
Allen Park, Michigan.

*For further information on Project Angel Tree®, a Ministry of Prison Fellowship, telephone toll-free (1) (800) 398-HOPE or (1) (703) 478-0100, extension 634.

GIVING FOR FUN

Throughout the year our two children, ages five and seven, receive $1.50 allowance each week. Fifty cents of their allowance is theirs to keep and spend, fifty cents is their church contribution, and fifty cents goes into their "savings" banks. At Christmastime, they take their year's savings and purchase gifts.

Last year, after everything was said and done, our daughter gave me a big hug and said, "You know, Mommy, it sure is fun giving presents to people!" My prayer is that in this age of self-gratification my children will learn that it is truly more blessed to give than to receive.

Tina Briley
resides in
Corpus Christi, Texas.

I love the holidays!

I hate the holidays!

I am a Christmas contradiction. I'm up with excitement and then down with disappointment. I'm up with anticipation and then down with depression. I'm up with . . . well, you get the idea. I'm on my seasonal seesaw. My teeter-totter partner is my own Currier-and-Ives expectations.

Ever notice in those Currier and Ives pictures how even in frigid weather the cows are contented? They willingly pose next to the wood for the fireplace, which is neatly stacked next to the house. While Bossy grins, Junior is shown joyfully skipping out to bring Mother dear kindling for the stove.

I don't have a cow, but I do have a dog. Pumpkin refuses to go outside if it's damp. She has an aversion to moist feet. She will sit for days with her paws crossed, waiting for the sun or wind to dry up the ground. No way is she going to pose willingly by a wet wood pile.

Of course, that would be difficult anyway since we don't have any wood—that is, unless I hike five miles to the woods and gnaw off a few branches. Oh, well, our fireplace stays cleaner that way.

I tried to imagine our Junior skipping joyfully toward a task outside in inclement weather. Ha! I think Junior caught Pumpkin's malady.

No matter how I try, I can't seem to cram my family onto the front of one of those cards.

I don't know why I can't remember, from one Christmas season to the next, that Currier and Ives is an unattainable height. Every Christmas, I want my house to be picture perfect. Ha! I can't achieve that in a nonholiday time, much less in a season with so many added demands.

I imagine white birch logs (cut by me in our back 40—feet, that is) snuggled in a handwoven basket (I designed) placed next to the hearth. The blazing fire invites guests to warm in our candle-lit (all hand-dipped by me) dining room. I would serve a

Reprinted with permission from *Normal Is Just a Setting On Your Dryer*, by Focus on the Family Publishing. Copyright © 1993, Patsy Clairmont.

REMEMBER

gourmet dinner for 30, followed by strolling musicians playing Handel's "Messiah." All this would take place in my 10-by-12 dining area.

When I have such unreasonable goals, I end up with a high frustration level and a frazzled nervous system. Then I find myself in last-minute panic spurts, trying to excuse, hide, and disguise all my unfinished projects.

One year we decided to write Noel in lights on our house. We started late and finished only half the project because of bad weather. That left a multi-colored NO flashing on our rooftop. We had fewer guests that year.

Usually, I wait too long to complete my shopping, leaving me victim to jangled nerves from holiday traffic, crowds, and check-out lines. People's personalities are seldom enhanced under pressure. Also, I tend to be more impulsive in my buying when I'm running late. I suffer from bargain whiplash trying to take advantage of all the Christmas markdowns. Too many last-minute purchases leave me holding the bag . . . and it's full of bills. The bills then pile up in my emotions, leaving me feeling spent.

Also, during the holiday hoopla I seem to get bit by the bug. No, not the flu bug; the love bug. I fall into the trap of thinking everyone is going to get along. Give me a break! How unrealistic to believe relatives and friends, some of whom have never hit it off, would suddenly become seasonal sidekicks! I'm learning there are those who believe "Ho, Ho, Ho" is something you do strictly in your garden and has nothing to do with exhibiting a merry heart.

Another habit I have is wanting everyone to love the gifts I give them as much as I did when I selected them. I'm into applause and appreciation. Here's the problem: I live with three guys (one husband and two sons), and they only applaud silly things like grand slam home runs in the World Series, touchdowns in the final seconds of the Super Bowl, or when I fix dinner and they can tell what it is.

They don't show the same enthusiasm for my gifts—like the nifty button extenders, the monogrammed electric socks, or the fuchsia-colored long johns I wrapped for them. I realize my gifts are . . . uh . . . distinctive, but I want them to be memorable. My guys agree they have been.

The Family Treasury of Great Holiday Ideas

Well, there it is, my Christmas confession. Maybe some of you can identify with part, if not all, of my seasonal seesaw. Come join me in entering into the holidays without the teeter and totter in our emotions. Here's how:

1. Set more-sane house goals. Better to plan less and accomplish more than to fall short of your ideal and start your holidays feeling disappointed.

2. Shop early, and buy a couple of generic emergency gifts. (Unlike fuchsia underwear, a box of fine chocolates holds general appeal.)

3. Settle on a reasonable budget before going into the stores to prevent falling victim to strong sales tactics (which include Christmas mood music that plays on our nostalgia, sale-sign seduction, and plastic explosives in the form of credit cards).

4. Sow the seeds of goodwill, but don't expect every "Scrooge" in your Christmas circle to embrace your efforts . . . or you, for that matter. Don't snowball your own emotions by expecting love from people who can't give it. (History in a relationship is usually a good benchmark of his or her ability.)

5. Seek some silence. Balance your busyness with moments of meditation. Don't allow all the flashing lights on the outside to distract you from the inner light of His presence. Even a short silence each day will give a greater semblance of order to your emotions and schedule.

Set goals, shop early, settle budget, sow goodwill,
seek silence,
and don't forget to
SIMPLY CELEBRATE!

Ways to celebrate simply:

Make a snow angel, drink eggnog, write a forgotten friend, decorate a snowman, go caroling in your neighborhood, feed the birds, bake apples, watch the movies *Heidi* and *Little Women*, write a poem, cut out cookies, share tea with a friend, frame an old snapshot, hug a child, hug an oldster, read the Christmas story out loud, and sing Happy Birthday to Jesus.

Patsy Clairmont
is a popular speaker and best-selling author of
God Uses Cracked Pots
(Focus on the Family Publishing).
She resides in Brighton, Michigan.

REMEMBER

Instead of using postage to send cards to church members, our church sets up boxes in the foyer divided into sections for each letter of the alphabet. Members hand out cards there, and check for cards for themselves as well. Everyone is encouraged to use the postage money they would have spent for the missionary offering.

Adopt two or three (or more!) missionary families from your church and write them during this season. They often feel the most lonely for their families and their country when they are gone over the holidays. Choose families that have children about your own children's ages and have your children include notes or pictures.

Michelle C. Hooks
resides in
Apopka, Florida.

WHO WILL MAKE THE LIGHTS SPARKLE?

When I was a child, I thought Christmas never came soon enough. I anxiously awaited the first set of lights to appear or for the smell of pine as my grandfather carried in the still-growing evergreen tree for us to decorate. Every moment was magic and it made the lights sparkle.

I never dreamed that Christmas could become a chore, a drudgery, and a burden, but that is exactly what happened when I became a parent and—not by choice—the family's "Christmas magician."

Suddenly it was up to me to decorate our home, bake cookies, buy and wrap the perfect gift for everyone, address and write witty Christmas cards, and then wait breathlessly for the season to arrive. And trust me—I was out of breath, and out of joy and excitement, for the holiday I had always loved best.

Christmas had become a major production that began six months ahead of time. Christmas decorations were on sale along with the back-to-school supplies. We hurried through

The Family Treasury of Great Holiday Ideas

Halloween and almost ignored Thanksgiving. The Christmas rush started earlier and earlier each year.

I watched the crowds as they circled the malls draped in silver and tinsel, with Elvis Christmas carols booming, and I never saw a smiling face. I know the shepherds came with haste but I don't believe they meant to create the Christmas rush.

I'd buy every holiday publication offered at the newsstands. Yes, I did want to make those lace angels and red velvet bows to redo the tree this year. Yes, I could frost our ginger-bread house to look like Disney World. Why I bet I could even needle-point all eight reindeer on coasters in time. And I'd order Christmas tree toilet paper. That was just the right touch.

Touched is right—I was losing my mind. I'd work all hours of the night so that everything would be perfect. After all, I could sleep in January. I could never understand why my husband didn't get more (or even somewhat) enthusiastic about the holidays. Okay, so I was exhausted and grumpy, the kids were on a sugar high, and we were broke. Did that give him any right to be downright negative?

When I read about a workshop called "How to Deal with Christmas Stress" I said, "Enough is enough!" Christmas stress should be a contradiction in terms. I evaluated how we were observing the birth of a child born in a very humble stable. We had lost sight of what was meaningful and important. I wanted to see Christmas through the eyes of a child again. I wanted the lights to sparkle.

Then I found a book, *Unplug the Christmas Machine*, that has since changed the way my family approaches and celebrates Christmas. It is full of ideas about how to return to a simpler, more joy-filled holiday.

Ninety percent of what we do at Christmas is for children. But, contrary to popular belief, kids do not want a perfect Victorian tree, a formal dinner party, or exhausted, frantic parents.

According to *Unplug the Christmas Machine*, they want:
1. Relaxed and loving time with the family.
2. Realistic expectations about gifts.
3. An evenly paced holiday season
4. Strong family traditions.

So now our family is striving to make some gradual changes

REMEMBER

and restructure our Christmas. We love our families dearly but we were going to four different celebrations on Christmas Eve and Christmas Day. Inevitably, the first snow or ice storm hit right about then so we'd often be taking our lives in our hands.

Now we've asked one side of the family to celebrate a day or two after Christmas, and we visit with just one family on Christmas Day. That leaves Christmas Eve for our children's Christmas program and a candlelight buffet at home with just our own family. It's a new tradition that we treasure.

Another aspect of Christmas has often disturbed me. What do we give our children for Christmas gifts? The answer in far too many cases is war toys! How does a gift that teaches destruction and death honor the birth of the Prince of Peace?

We are raising children who are being desensitized to the horrors of war and who seek to solve problems with guns and battle.

For younger children, consider giving playdough, simple musical instruments, puppets, dolls, Legos, art supplies, records, trucks, puzzles, flashlights, magnets, fire engines, easels and paint, building blocks, and books.

For older children, think about magic kits, sports equipment, hobby kits, radios, cameras, fun clothing, lessons of any kind, models, board games, tapes, sleeping bags, wild jewelry, and books.

Of course the gift they want dearly is the gift of your time. One day as I was racing around the house, putting up the decorations and running off to a meeting, my son asked me to play a game with him. In my rush I said, "Can't you play with one of your toys?" But his response opened my eyes and my heart.

"But don't you know that no toy is gooder than a mother?" he said.

Plan the events for December to include the children. They don't want to spend the month with babysitters. Church and school festivities are important and provide good family time. Give up the office party and do something as a family. Go to the tuba Christmas concert or on a sleigh ride; volunteer to carol for shut-ins or open your home to someone or some family in need.

Traditions—without them our lives would be as shaky as a

The Family Treasury of Great Holiday Ideas

fiddler on the roof. Why do we do so much of what we do? Because of tradition. Traditions are wonderful, comfortable, and comforting. They can also become a checklist of obligations.

When I was a child my mother always baked cutout Christmas cookies and let all four of us do our own cookie decorating. She would make frosting in every hue, including the bright blue we loved even before the Cookie Monster. The entire kitchen was white with flour and the floor crunched with sugar and chocolate jimmies for days.

However, I've discovered that I hate being the mother part of this tradition. I can't cut out a decent cookie for love nor money. No matter how hard I try, I always cut the dough too thin (the only thin thing in my life!). My cookies always broke when we tried to frost them. I hate making dough. The whole tradition made me ill.

I stuck with it until I thought hard about what a tradition should do for you. This one did not give me a warm, happy feeling.

When I told this to a group of friends, they introduced me to a grandmother who loved to cut out cookies and didn't have any young grandchildren. She offered to be our Cookie Grandma and for the last five years she has made cookies and sent them over for the children to decorate. Now mind you, I don't mind the crunchy floor, it's just the baking process I abhor.

So we still have cookies, the kids still get to lick the frosting bowl, and we have a wonderful, dear new friend. The last few years our boys have even volunteered to help her with the baking.

Not all traditions are dealt with that easily and happily. But since there is only one fruitcake in the world that is passed from family to family, I'm going to wait for my turn. We do cheat a bit and make our gingerbread house out of graham crackers and leftover Halloween candy. No, orange and black don't look terrific at Christmas, so I buy generic gum drops and lollipops. The children do the decorating and it's the last decoration I take down after the holiday. It truly is a work of love and creativity.

If a tradition is a burden, think it over, change it, alter it, or forget it. Children will take hold of a new tradition and guard it closely. You might have a special holiday breakfast, host a tree

REMEMBER

219

lighting party, light an Advent wreath each evening or fix a food basket for the hungry to teach the joy of giving.

It's time to take control of your holidays. Don't let them control you. And watch how the lights will sparkle as the true joy and meaning of Christmas return.

Mary Liebetrau
resides in
West Bend, Indiana.

A New Holiday

My father's death at Christmastime nearly twelve years ago changed our holiday dinners forever. He was a patriarchal force at the head of the table and his death interrupted our family traditions.

Perhaps out of my own sense of "homelessness," I scouted through a rough neighborhood of our city distributing posters announcing that there would be food and coffee at a busy corner one Christmas Eve following my father's death. There we were, Mom and I and other helpers, handing out hot coffee and bag lunches when most families were home enjoying the evening as it was meant to be enjoyed.

Since that Christmas Eve we have found our way to new levels of celebrating and enjoying the season. And we have talked more about reaching out to the homeless with our simple gifts.

If your family is experiencing a loss during this joyful time of year, consider welcoming into your family those for whom loss is an everyday way of life.

Timothy Schultz
resides in
Atlantic City, New Jersey.

The Family Treasury of Great Holiday Ideas

When we focus all our attention on what we hope to receive for Christmas, we miss an important part of the season. Begin a tradition in your family of doing something special each holiday season to give away your Christmas.

- Take a basket of Christmas gifts to a family that's struggling financially.
- Offer to run holiday errands for a homebound person.
- Pack a box of Christmas goodies, and take it to the firefighters on duty Christmas Eve.
- Bake cookies with your children for the mail carrier and sanitation workers.
- Decorate the home of an elderly person. Help take down the decorations after Christmas.
- Give an anonymous gift of money to a needy family. Volunteer as a family to help at a soup kitchen for the homeless.
- Go caroling as a family at a nursing home or hospital. (Call before you go to get permission.)
- Bake double batches of Christmas goodies for friends who don't have time.

Kathy Peel
is a Contributing Editor to Family Circle *magazine. She has authored six books, including* Do Plastic Surgeons Take Visa? *(Word, 1992) and* The Stomach Virus and Other Forms of Family Bonding *(Word, 1993). She travels frequently, speaking at conferences and conventions.*

REMEMBER

THANKSGIVING EVE AT CHURCH

On Thanksgiving Eve our pastor held a private family candle
light communion. One family at a time entered the candleli
sanctuary and had prayer, Bible reading, and communion. I
was beautifully done. We were gracefully reminded that th
Lord should be at the center of every celebration.

Lisa D. Hughes
resides in
Phoenix, Arizona.

HANDS ACROSS THE TABLE

American holidays are strongly laced with family togetherness
Having been foreign missionaries for most of our adult lives
and having no biological children, we have learned to fin
family wherever we are.

At present our lives are entwined with international students
helping them adjust to a new culture, learn English, and de
velop friendships with Americans, all for the ultimate purpos
of sharing Jesus.

Since we are involved in an international conference ove
Thanksgiving weekend, we celebrate with our internationa
"family" Wednesday evening, combining a dinner and Bibl
study.

Early arrivals like to migrate to the kitchen to watch th
dissection of the turkey, many never having tasted it before
When most have arrived, song sheets are handed out, and afte
some explanation of words, we sing "Come, ye thankful peopl
come."

Across the hall in a second apartment (part of which w
subrent), candles are lit on the tables with festive place settings
The guests fill their plates from the buffet in the first apartmen
and fill the tables across the hall. There is an explanation abou

why turkey, corn and lima beans, cranberry salad, and pumpkin pie are traditional, amid many comments and laughter.

After dessert and coffee, more papers are passed out giving a brief history of Thanksgiving, appropriate Scriptures on giving thanks, songs, and then a chance for everyone to verbalize their own thanks. Usually *everyone* says something, even if in halting English. (We often have visiting parents of students.)

The evening ends with a wonderful sense of good will and comradeship.

Pete and Mim Stern
reside in
Philadelphia, Pennsylvania.

KERNELS OF THANKS

On each plate set on our Thanksgiving table are several kernels of corn. Before eating we take turns going around the table saying something we are thankful for, for each kernel of corn we have. As we say each thing, we drop a kernel in a basket on the table. It's a great way to review the year and be thankful even for things that happened a while ago, and also to share those blessings with family members.

Becky S. Shipp
resides in
Flint, Michigan.

REMEMBER

Sometimes memories serve to fuel the creation of other memories. I don't know if we were inspired by *It's a Wonderful Life* or just by the spirit of the season, but several years ago my home church created a game called "Angels and Mortals." Because some of my family's fondest memories have resulted from the game, we now play it each year.

Unlike most games, anyone who plays "Angels and Mortals" is a winner. The rules are simple: We put each one's name on a slip of paper and then place the names in a hat. Each person draws a name and becomes that person's "secret angel."

Over the course of the holiday season, each "angel" must secretly do nice things for his or her "mortal." At the end of the holidays we have a party and tell each other who our mortal was. In addition to being great fun, this game gives us a sense of just how thankful we should be for the unseen things real angels do for us each day.

Twila Paris
is an acclaimed singer
and songwriter of Christian music.

From: *Making A Christmas Memory*.
By: Twila Paris with Jeanie Price. Copyright © 1990.
Used by permission of Tyndale House Publishers, Inc.
All rights reserved.

The lion and lamb, symbol of peace, is the emblem of our church, so each year we try to find Christmas cards depicting a lion and lamb. Over the years we have amassed quite a collection with many unusual scenes. We always save a card to add to our Christmas treasures and each year we enjoy looking at the many varied scenes from jungle settings to snowy landscapes, yet all symbolic of "Peace on Earth."

Mickey and William Harris
reside in
Escatawpa, Mississippi.

AN ADVENT SUPPER

The board of education at our church has for years sponsored a family soup and sandwich supper to precede the first Wednesday Advent church service. A craft hour follows the meal and then the church service starts at 7:00 P.M.

The craft project consists of something that would enhance our Advent season—a wreath, banner, decoration, and so on. Usually there is a family project to work on together and also easy projects that young children can accomplish alone. A small fee is charged for the meal and the craft to cover expenses.

Barbara Johnson
resides in
Eau Claire, Wisconsin.

REMEMBER

To remember whose birthday we are celebrating, we use a small gift-wrapped box that has a hole on the top. We set the box by our nativity scene on a shelf. For three to four weeks before Christmas members of our family drop spare change into the box as a gift to Jesus. The Sunday before Christmas our special offering is taken to church and given as a birthday present to Jesus.

Chris Brown
resides in
Jones, Michigan.

Cup of Cheer

Each member of our family has a hot chocolate mug with a brightly colored Christmas design on it. At the beginning of December we make hot chocolate, pour it into our mugs, add little marshmallows, and sprinkle colored sprinkles on top. We stir the delightful concoction with candy canes! This simple tradition, relished by our children, will be a memory that will last for a lifetime.

Judy Senne
resides in
Kansas City, Missouri.

THE FAMILY OF GOD

Visit morning and evening Sunday services of several different denominations. This may prove to be the best part of the holidays, as you are reminded that the family of God extends outside your own church and circle of friends. (Someone who is living alone or feeling lonesome might find this activity particularly satisfying. Why not invite them along?)*

THE FAMILY THAT READS TOGETHER

Set aside a time for family Bible reading every day in December, maybe right after breakfast or supper. You can make sure preschoolers don't feel left out by giving them a beautiful bookmark to mark the correct passage. Here are some daily suggestions:*

Nov. 30—Isaiah 42:1-9
Dec. 2—Isaiah 55
Dec. 4—Luke 1:26-38
Dec. 6—John 1:11-18
Dec. 8—Malachi 3:1-4
Dec. 10—Mark 1:1-13
Dec. 12—Isaiah 52:1-6
Dec. 14—Luke 1:5-25
Dec. 16—Luke 1:39-56
Dec. 18—Luke 1:57-80
Dec. 20—Revelation 21:1-7
Dec. 22—Revelation 1:10-18

Dec. 1—Psalm 89:1-29
Dec. 3—Isaiah 35
Dec. 5—John 1:1-10
Dec. 7—Micah 5:2
Dec. 9—Matthew 1:18-25
Dec. 11—Isaiah 40:1-11
Dec. 13—Isaiah 9:2-7
Dec. 15—Luk 2:8-20
Dec. 17—Jeremiah 33:7-16
Dec. 19—Isaiah 61
Dec. 21—Matthew 2:1-12

REMEMBER

"I can't wait 'til Christmas!" the children exclaim. It often seems a *long* time until Christmas comes, especially when store decorations go up right after Halloween. To help shorten the wait, in our house, we try to have "minicelebrations" throughout December.

Early in the month we have a children's Christmas cookie decorating party for our two girls and their friends. We bake the cookies ahead of time, color canned frosting in several colors, and stock up on sprinkles. The children decorate one big cookie for their snack and one to take home. I read a Christmas story to them and then we play a few games like "Hunt for the Christmas Ornament," "Toss the Candy into the Muffin Tin," or "Pin the Nose on Rudolph."

Our girls, ages seven and ten, enjoy learning how people in other countries celebrate Christmas. We celebrate St. Nicholas Day on 6 December by putting small presents and Christmas candies in their dolls' shoes. They each get to open a present that day, a Christmas coloring or craft book, paper dolls, or a book.

On 13 December, St. Lucia's Day, our oldest daughter dressed in a white nightgown with a red sash, wearing a cardboard and felt crown of candles that she had made. She served us cinnamon rolls, made the day before. We read parts of *Kirsten's Surprise* by Janet Shaw, 1986, Pleasant Company, a Swedish Christmas story. By having these fun times to look forward to, the long wait seemed shorter to them.

Janet M. Blair
resides in
Ansonia, Connecticut.

The Family Treasury of Great Holiday Ideas

Preparations for Christmas used to start in our house about October, at least the most meaningful one I can remember after these sixty years.

At our daily evening devotional time, Daddy would have our family start memorizing the account of Christ's birth as recorded in Matthew or Luke, alternating one or the other each year. By the time Christmas arrived, we were able to quote the Scripture account by heart.

This was so meaningful to me as a child that my husband and I carried on that same tradition with our own five children. Our firstborn could recite Luke 2:1-20 when he was four years old.

Now we have twelve grandchildren, some of them teenagers. Last year two of our daughters and their families shared Christmas Day with us. At our traditional time for devotions, three generations rejoiced together at the incomparable Scripture account of Christ's coming as Savior, through the reciting of the various passages by memory.

Rachael O. Picazo
resides in
Morehead, Kentucky.

LETTERS TO MY SONS

At the holiday time I write a letter to each of my boys. In the letter I review things that have happened over the year, accomplishments that they have had, sometimes even their shoe size or batting average. I also tell them again how proud of them I am and how much I love them. I let them read the letter and then I put it away. I had originally thought I would give back the letters when they turned eighteen. I have decided, however, to continue the tradition until each one is out of college.

Diana M. White
resides in
Scotts Valley, California.

REMEMBER

When our children were small, we started a tradition of the ten days of Christmas. My husband Tim and I would set up our nativity scene in a prominent spot. Then on the 14th of December (ten days before Christmas Eve), we would begin special devotions: Each devotion centered on a figure in the manger scene and always came back to the theme of Jesus' birth, God's special gift to us. Each child was allowed to hold the figure and pass it on to another. The figure of Baby Jesus would be last, with Tim emphasizing the celebration of Christ's birthday on the following day. Our children really enjoyed this for many seasons. If for some reason we forgot, they would remind us!

As the children reached their teen years, we were fortunate enough to go away for a family holiday at Christmas. About seven days before Christmas Day, we began our "special" devotions. This time we read from books like *How Silently, How Silently* (J. Bayley), *The Best Christmas Pageant Ever* (B. Robinson), and *God Came Near* (M. Lucado). Then after discussion and prayer each person was allowed to take one item from their Christmas stocking. Stocking stuffers thus became an important "treat." Even though our family is grown, this sharing of stocking stuffers is still an important holiday time. We look forward to this expression of our love for each other and for Jesus, God's ultimate present to us all.

Sheila Hudson
resides in
Athens, Georgia.

CHRISTMAS CARD LONGEVITY

Beautiful (and expensive) Christmas cards have such a short life that I am always delighted to hear of people who have found ways to extend the pleasure they bring.

When I was a child, Mother invented games for us to play with the avalanche of cards that came to our house. We would tax our brains to learn the signatures then see who could do best at naming the sender just by looking at the front of the card. It became harder and harder as the pile grew larger.

Or, one child would pose as a figure from one of the cards, with everyone else trying to guess which one he had chosen to portray. No question about it—we enjoyed those cards for weeks. By the time we tired of them they were almost too worn to recycle in traditional ways.

Friends who have received my Christmas card poems tell me a variety of ways they have extended their life. One used hers as a Bible bookmark, another as a tree ornament, another as guest-room reading material.

All of my family look forward to the greetings sent each year by an artistically talented cousin. Painstakingly, with dainty lettering and intricate cutwork, she creates these cards, one by one. I'm sure we all cherish them, but one recipient does more. As Christmas approaches, she takes down her antique china from the plate rail in the dining room and displays the accumulated collection that now contains more than thirty beautiful works of art.

Among my acquaintances is a closet artist. Each year he selects the most beautiful card he has received that year and reproduces it in oils, in a size suitable for framing. Each Christmas season the regular pictures come down and his Christmas reproductions go up. Plagiarism? I think both the artist and the greeting card company would consider it an accolade.

Busy people sometimes don't give cards the attention they merit when they first arrive. One pastor's family saves the cards to savor one-a-day throughout the year, including the sender in their daily prayers. They do not concern themselves with selecting the most beautiful, nor creating a seasonal display, nor entertaining themselves with the cards. They concentrate on the sender.

Perhaps that response is the one most appropriate to the spirit of Christmas—that time when Love came to earth, to stay all year 'round.

Barbara Sutryn
resides in
Montoursville, Pennsylvania.

REMEMBER

A Tree Farm Outing

In our house everyone loves to participate when it is time to put up the Christmas tree. We've extended the excitement of that by going to a tree farm each year. There we walk through the vast selection of trees until we find the perfect one and Dad chops it down. After the tree has been put on the car, we warm up with hot chocolate, sometimes taking the hayride offered by the tree farm. Then, it's back home to trim our tree and enjoy some eggnog and Christmas cookies.

Christine Beckett
resides in
Matawan, New Jersey.

Stars in Your Eyes

On a clear night, bundle up in warm clothes and go outside to look at the stars. In the dark, talk about the star of Bethlehem and the coming of the Christ-child and his message of love. Go around the family circle and ask each to name one thing he remembers about Jesus' life and mission. See how many times you can go around the circle. Sit on a bench, blanket, or tarp and count stars.*

Sleep Under a Tree

Let the kids sleep in sleeping bags under the Christmas tree the night after Christmas. It's fun to look up through the branches toward the top of the tree, and to fall asleep with the soft glow of the tree lights. For safety, an adult should be sure to turn the lights off after the youngsters are asleep.*

A SPECIAL CHRISTMAS GAME

As a mother of two daughters it was important to me to start a tradition when they were very young that would go with them through the years. As we decorate the tree we choose ornaments that are special to us and hide them on the tree. Fraser fir trees are great because they allow you to tuck ornaments deep inside the tree. Thus begins our Special Christmas Game.

All the lights go out and we sit or lounge around the tree and try to find each other's ornaments! It's fun to search all over the tree for those special ornaments that mean so much to us. When the ornaments are found, one by one, a story is told about where each ornament came from and a very special Christmas memory is relived.

Toni Sims
resides in
Kosciusko, Mississippi.

CHRISTMAS READING

Since my husband and I have been married, we've made it a tradition to buy a new book each year that is focused on Christmas. Every December, we pull them all out and have a special time each day for reading and rereading them. There's a wide selection—children's, fiction, and so on—and we've enjoyed all of them.

Annette McEndarfer
resides in
Worcester, Massachusetts.

REMEMBER

When our son Jonathan was two years old, we received a lovely, hand-painted nativity set complete with people, stable animals, sheep, and camels. We would sit together as a family and read the Christmas story while moving the appropriate figurines into place. Each year Jonathan eagerly awaited the unpacking of the nativity set and we would again read the story of our Lord's birth and act it out with the figurines.

A few years later Brian was added to our family and I vividly remember the Christmas when he was two years old. When we unpacked the nativity set, Jonathan excitedly called out, "Brian come here, let me show you the story of baby Jesus!" As I watched, he told the story from memory and showed Brian what each piece was and the part it played in the story. He had some difficulty explaining the angel to a two year old who thought that anything with wings had to be a bird.

Day by day through each holiday season the nativity scene changes appearance as different family members arrange it while practicing the Christmas story. Those figurines now bear the evidence of being handled by young hands, but we don't treasure the nativity set for its physical beauty. Rather, we treasure it for what it has birthed in the hearts of our children and the precious gift from God that it represents.

Kelly Lutman
resides in
Lansing, Kansas.

My German grandmother used to tell me tales of all the ornaments on the tree. When my own three sons were old enough to comprehend their meanings, I told them the beloved stories, and now my grandchildren are enjoying them as well.

The star on top of the tree symbolizes the star of Bethlehem that shone, leading the three wise men to the stable where Jesus lay.

The lights are all the other stars twinkling in the sky.

The garland wraps around the tree like a mother's arms wrapped around her babe, loving and protecting it.

The round ornaments signify the earth that God created for man. The colors are different and each represents something special. Red is for Jesus' blood that was shed to redeem us. Blue is for the skies that glow by sunlight during the day and shimmer by moonlight during the night. Green is for the trees and plants that God created to provide food for us. Silver and gold are for the rich blessings that He has given us.

The tinsel glistens like little sparks of fire, like the fire Joseph probably made to keep Mary and Jesus warm.

And the tree itself is full of life, adorned, standing proudly and pointing to heaven where Jesus waits for us . . . the tree seems to say, "Happy Birthday, Jesus, Happy Birthday!"

Janet Smith
resides in
Sunnyvale, California.

GOD'S GREATEST GIFT

Each Christmas, we set out our nativity set and leave the baby Jesus wrapped. On Christmas Day, we let our little one unwrap the baby Jesus as we talk about God's gift to us—His Son.

Charlene L. Cragg
resides in
Moreno Valley, California.

REMEMBER

It can take me two full days to decorate our Christmas tree and about four hours just to put on the lights. I'm particular. So you can understand why my sister said things would have to change when my son was born—no way would my tree ever be the same again.

When my son's first Christmas rolled around—he was eleven months, walking quite well, and into everything—I decorated my tree as usual from the top down to just about his eye level. I gathered up all his stuffed animals that were relatively small and decorated them with Christmas ribbons and wreaths and then purchased some small Christmas teddies and reindeer (about six inches high). This menagerie hung on the lower limbs of the tree and Daniel spent his days arranging and rearranging them.

When he got older and I could have my whole tree back, we purchased another tree for upstairs. We decorated it with the original menagerie plus all Daniel's other stuffed animals.

Today we decorate our family tree together and Daniel is as particular as I about how things are arranged.

Roxanna T. Sieber
resides in
Villisca, Iowa.

CHRISTMAS IN MIAMI

How do you celebrate Christmas in Miami when the weather outside is 84 degrees? I turn the air conditioner way down, put on a sweater, and play Christmas carols on high. For an Ohio-born girl dreaming of a White Christmas, it's the best I can do.

Of course, then we celebrate the real reason for the season—that God came down to earth! That's why we love to celebrate! That's why we decorate our homes. It's an act of gratitude and worship. For me the Christmas tree is the crowning touch.

The Family Treasury of Great Holiday Ideas

Scripture says "the trees of the field shall clap their hands," and I want our tree to sparkle as a standing ovation to our dear Savior, Jesus.

Last December we had a tree trimming party and invited some friends who had not participated in our tradition because of their Jewish faith. They seemed pleased to be a part of the family gathering as we feasted on a sumptuous buffet of wassail, roasted tenderloin, cheese grits soufflé, and countless goodies.

After dinner, we all got to work decorating. I had to smile at all the action. All ages and shapes were bending and stretching around the tree, placing each ornament in just the right spot. Several grandmothers, playing artist, painted freshly baked gingerbread boys, dipping their brushes in cups of tinted frosting. Throughout the evening, the most action centered around the tarts and cakes on the dessert table! With Christmas carols playing softly, it was a happy scene.

Then at last, with satisfied tummies and warm hearts, we basked in the glow of our work of art, the Christmas tree. In that shining moment, I prayed silently that my Jewish friends would know our love for them, and perhaps catch a glimpse of God's great salvation:

> "For unto us a child is born,
> Unto us a son is given,
> And His name shall be called Wonderful Counselor,
> the Mighty God, the Everlasting Father,
> the Prince of Peace."

Marabel Morgan
is the author of The Total Woman *(Revell)*
and other best-sellers. She resides
in Miami, Florida.

Taken from: Marabel Morgan, *The Total Woman Cookbook*, Fleming H. Revell, a division of Baker Book House Company, Copyright © 1980.

REMEMBER

When our two children were about six and eight years old, we began a tradition rather accidentally. On the Saturday I planned to bake holiday cookies my children wanted to invite four neighborhood children over to help. I agreed (wondering where my sanity was), and soon I was overseeing six little people as they measured and stirred and mixed and licked. I've forgotten how many different kinds of cookies and candies we made that day, but I've never forgotten the fun it was. At one point I instructed my son Darrin to "stir it 'til the lumps are out." He looked at me so innocently and asked, "Can't I just eat the lumps out?"

Kids' Baking Day happened one Saturday every December until my daughter was a senior in high school. By then I had been retired from the kitchen and the kids had taken over the baking. Sure there was flour in places where flour doesn't belong and batter on the cupboard doors, but the laughter and good times will always be a part of our memories. We look at the pictures in the family album and remember those wonderful Kids' Baking Days.

Judy Lovitt
resides in
Ogden, Utah.

CHRISTMAS IN THE 1920s AND 30s
(as I remember it)

"They're going to build a toyland town all around the Christmas tree." Surely the composer of "Santa Claus Is Coming to Town" must have taken his inspiration from Baltimore in the 1920s and 30s. Everyone who could, had a "Christmas Garden" at the base of his Christmas tree. We were no different.

After Thanksgiving dinner was cleared away, we kids (my brother Wilson and I) were banished from the living room (and often the dining room) until Christmas morning. What interest-

The Family Treasury of Great Holiday Ideas

ing and curiosity-arousing sounds came from there! But we were never given a hint of what was going on.

You see, there was a friendly rivalry between my dad and Mr. Baum who lived two houses down. They tried to outdo each other with their gardens. If we knew what was going on, we could have easily let it slip in a bragging session with Billy or Bobby Baum.

Although the theme changed from year to year, there was one constant—a model train that invariably derailed in the tunnel through the man-made mountains or on the far side of the garden (flush with the wall four feet away). We had an "O" gauge in the early days, but when Wilson was old enough he *made* from kits an "HO" set. (The only way you could get them was to make them.)

Wilson used matchsticks for the railroad ties and he also made his own houses and stations. Once he used plans published in *Better Homes and Gardens* to make a darling little house. That year he also made a factory and a station, all to the HO scale.

But back to Dad's garden. We had a fountain that ran spasmodically using recirculated water. That was always in the city square. But one year Dad added a waterfall and stream that ran the length of the garden (usually fifteen feet, the length of the living room). He drilled two holes in the living room floor to run pipes from the basement laundry tub and back again. (Wonder what the person who bought the house thought of those two holes in the living room floor!) Whenever anyone came to see the garden, one of us had to run downstairs to turn on the water to the shouts of, "Too much! Little more! Hold it there!" That year Dad had outsmarted Mr. Baum for sure.

Another time that he thought he had outsmarted him was the year of the amusement park. But Mr. Baum had come up with the same idea. Of course, Wilson and I thought ours was the best by far. And, of course, the Baum boys thought theirs was best.

I don't remember details from theirs, but ours had a playground with swings that swung, seesaws that seesawed and a merry-go-round that twirled, all with tiny, tiny dolls on them. I was "allowed" to dress the dolls although I didn't know what they were for until Christmas morning.

REMEMBER

There were other moving things but I can't remember what they were. Except the roller coaster! (In Baltimore this was known as a "racer dip.") Dad had gotten thin strips of wood to build it from leftovers from my uncle's cigar box factory. I can remember Wilson bringing them home on the streetcar.

A little car with more of the dolls in it climbed the long ascent to the top of the roller coaster, and took off from there! And I mean took off! One time it went sailing across the living room. (Dad never could figure how to slow that thing down, and along with it the swing, seesaw, and so one that sent dolls into space until he thought to glue them to their seats.)

One time the preacher came to "see the garden." After a demonstration of the marvels of our amusement park, he took an envelope out of his pocket and wrote on it, "RIDE AT YOUR OWN RISK!" and stuck it on the side of the roller coaster.

One year we had a moving roadway that carried little cars along. That became a source of great amusement when someone set the rheostat too fast.

In those days homes weren't decorated. People would put their trees near a window so that the lights could be seen at night. Several blocks down the street next to us there was a row of homes with sun parlors (windowed rooms attached to the front of the houses). The people who lived there would all put their trees in the sun parlor. We would take a walk on Christmas night just to see those lighted trees. To my young mind they were thousands of jewels sparkling in the night.

Those who lived in the city would put their gardens next to the window because the sidewalks came right up to the house. They would enjoy watching folks as they walked up to the window to see the garden. Often, seeing people looking in, they would start the train running. (Almost everyone had a train.) One of our week-after-Christmas activities was to ride around town on the streetcar and see all the trees in people's houses.

But not only private homes had Christmas gardens. Most of the fire stations also had them. The firefighters would park one or more of the engines outside the station (sometimes starting in the summer) and spend their spare time creating lavish gardens. In the 1950s and 60s one engine house had the four seasons depicted. For winter they had skiers going down a slope (they had learned how to control the speed) and in the

The Family Treasury of Great Holiday Ideas

summer section they had a drive-in movie using a small screen TV. Another station had a harbor scene with a ferryboat going back and forth and other ships coming and going. Usually you had to wait your turn to see these creations from the firefighters.

Much later when I married, our first Christmas "tree" was a branch cut off my mother's large tree and stuck in a jar of water. Our "garden" consisted of some houses cut from cereal boxes and set at the base of the "tree" on the game table. As the years rolled by and the children came, we had more traditional gardens, but nothing could compare with the ones of my childhood.

Margaret L. Matthews
resides in
Columbia, South Carolina.

AFTER THE KIDS GO TO BED

This is a simple holiday idea that is so obvious and yet for some reason my husband and I didn't take time to do this for years. After we put the children to bed, we turn off the television, put on some Christmas music, and turn off the other room lights. We sit and enjoy a warm drink, watch the pretty Christmas tree lights, and talk.

Kimberly Miller Wentworth
resides in
Colbert, Georgia.

REMEMBER

A Time to Enjoy

Each Christmas season we begin giving our gifts about a week before Christmas. When the children were young and received a lot of gifts we began this tradition by giving one gift each day starting about one week before Christmas. Even now as teenagers our children so look forward to receiving these gifts and are able to take time to enjoy them more. On Christmas day there is not a mad rush to open gifts—and not enjoy them.

Donna M. Hoult
resides in
Philadelphia, Pennsylvania.

The Play's the Thing!

When our children were small we always met at my sister's house on Christmas Eve. Grandparents on both sides were there too. One Christmas the children were so excited they were distracting us as we did last-minute preparations for the meal. I suggested they go downstairs and prepare to act out the nativity scene for us after supper, before we opened gifts.

Not only did they do a great job that year, but it became a family tradition. As they got older they even wrote their own stories and acted them out as plays. This tradition is spreading to the next generation as we are now the grandparents.

Mildred S. Barton
resides in
Anderson, South Carolina.

THE JOURNEY TO BETHLEHEM

Make a wall map of Joseph and Mary's journey from Nazareth to Bethlehem showing the route they may have taken: villages along the way; rivers, lakes, and mountains; and estimated number of miles between places. Children can even clip pictures from magazines or Christmas greeting cards to depict the scene more graphically. If the family enjoys this project, continue with a map showing the flight to Egypt. Read the Bible accounts to get as much information as you can for accuracy.*

A SUNRISE PICNIC

Establish an annual sunrise picnic some weekend morning during the holiday season. Take along bacon, eggs, potatoes, an old frying pan, a coffee percolator you don't care about, and plastic dishes and utensils. The kids can gather twigs and sticks to build a fire while adults peel potatoes, prepare the coffee, and set the table. After breakfast there will be woods and pleasant trails to investigate and beautiful bird songs and squirrel and chipmunk antics to enjoy.*

COME HOME FOR CHRISTMAS

Coming home for Christmas will cost much more for larger families, but holiday separations mean there is a vacuum in the heart, a small sad feeling that will not go away because someone is missing. One suggestion is for all families to covenant together to put away twenty dollars a week (or per month) for a holiday reunion the next year. If there's an accountant in the family, perhaps the money each month could be sent to him or her to be put in an interest-bearing account. If the plan works, and everyone wants to try it again, family members can take turns hosting so nobody has the burden over and over.*

*From: *Great Christmas Ideas.*
By: Alice Chapin Copyright © 1992.
Used by permission of Tyndale House Publishers, Inc.
All rights reserved.

REMEMBER

243

For years the entire family would attend Christmas Eve services at our church. However, as grandchildren began to arrive, at least one adult would not be able to share in the service in order to stay home with the children.

Since 1966 we have held our own Christmas Eve candle lighting service. The service begins with Grandpa Clarence offering prayer and reading those passages from the Bible telling of the birth of Christ. Each person's candle is then lit, and we all join in singing "Happy Birthday, Jesus," followed by Christmas carols. A sumptuous meal follows.

Clarence Blasier
enjoyed a successful business career before
rededicating his life to Jesus Christ in 1981.
Since then he has compiled, among others,
The Golden Treasury of Bible Wisdom
(Barbour Books).

JUST WAIT UNTIL DARK!

On Christmas Eve my husband and I and our two children wait just until dark and then we pile in the car and drive all over town to see our favorite lights. Afterward, at home, we have homemade oyster stew and crackers and hot cocoa or spice tea. When we're finished, we light candles, turn off the lights, and sing (individually or all together) our favorite Christmas carols and hymns *while recording ourselves*. We are sometimes serious and sometimes silly. Then one of us reads the birth of Christ from the Bible and we pray. The children are then allowed to open one gift before going to bed.

Tacey Nobles
resides in
Casper, Wyoming.

The Family Treasury of Great Holiday Ideas

Music has always been a part of Christmas at the Donaldsons'. As a youngster I enjoyed listening to the cousins join together to create a miniconcert for my grandparents. My father, aunt, and grandmother took turns at the piano and my mother and uncle would read a poem or short story.

Years have passed but the tradition has carried on. The younger generation now does all the planning and work as they share their God-given talents. The "Donaldson 5" plus spouses join their voices in singing favorite Christmas carols and my father plays his favorite hymns on the organ. There are many surprises as well as new music combinations are tried. An attempt at a flute, saxophone, and french horn trio and a guitar duet of "Jingle Bells" have been, needless to say, entertaining.

Thank You, God, for the talents You have given our family. Most of all, thank You for Your Son Jesus. He is the reason we celebrate and carry on the tradition.

Bethel Donaldson
resides in
Ogema, Wisconsin.

A Story to Remember

I wanted my children to anticipate the holidays while they remember the real reason for the season. Last fall we memorized one verse each week of Luke, chapter 2. When the holidays arrived my four year old and two year old could recite the Christmas story straight from God's Word! As they recited Luke's account at each family gathering, Christ became the focus for all of us. The children's self-esteem was boosted as both felt such a sense of accomplishment.

Kay Fuller
resides in
Forest City, Iowa.

REMEMBER

In our family we get together on the Friday night before Christmas. Previously we have drawn names and bought a gift for one person only. We gather at my house for the gift exchange and food. We enjoy a traditional South Texas feast of hot tamales, pinto beans, chips and dips, and sweets. At this gathering we take hundreds of photos. We have made many memories over the years and the photos bring back precious loved ones no longer with us and how we all looked "back then." We also keep a guest book each year and everyone signs in, even the little ones!

Zula Shenk
resides in
Robstown, Texas.

CHRISTMAS EVE POTLUCK

We all meet after church on Christmas Eve and share a potluck dinner. After eating and visiting we have our most meaningful event of the evening. Each family shares something that is on their hearts. For example, one family does a silly skit, one sings, one shares some Scripture verses. My father always shares the story of Christ's birth and then he talks a little to the grandchildren about keeping Christ first during these hard years. After all the presentations we sing "Happy Birthday" to Jesus and have a piece of His birthday cake. The children then exchange gifts. With such a big family—six children, all married, and eleven grandchildren—we are thankful we can all be together to have such a great time in Jesus.

Sharon E. Jacobson
resides in
Hitchcock, Texas.

A Christmas Prayer

To help our young children develop a spirit of thankfulness, each night during the month of December we have a special time of prayer. We begin our time by turning off the lights and lighting several candles. We stand in a circle holding hands (or a child) and thank the Father for several things and then for His Son. We blow out the candles and the children then go to bed with good, loving thoughts.

Evangelistic Christmas Party

Every year we host or assist in an evangelistic Christmas party. What better time of the year to gather children together and share with them the true message of the holiday! The party includes games, songs, a Bible story (a presentation of the Gospel), and a lot of fun. We have seen many children come to believe in the Lord Jesus as a result. Child Evangelism Fellowship is an excellent resource for such an endeavor.

Annette McEndarfer
resides in
Worcester, Massachusetts.

First One Up!

Since our children were small we have tried to focus on Jesus' birth and the true meaning of Christmas. Here's a tradition we began a few years ago. The first person who wakes up on Christmas morning—before he or she even gets out of bed—yells out loud, "Happy Birthday, Jesus!" Through the years it's always interesting to see who will be the first one to wake up. I don't think it's ever been Dad or Mom! The first year we did this I was surprised to hear my youngest who was four yell out bright and clear. She beat her two older brothers!

Jill Bomberger
resides in
Salem, Ohio.

REMEMBER

Last Christmas I couldn't afford to purchase any lavish gifts for my family, so I decided to put the emphasis on fun instead of money. I bought many small but useful inexpensive items, such as a calendar, boxes of stationery, a photo album, and so on. I didn't put name tags on any of the wrapped gifts. Each person chose a gift one at a time, and opened it. The next person could then choose whether or not to take that gift or pick a different one from the pile. When something you like is taken from you, and you have to choose a new gift all over again, you have to laugh about it.

Lisa D. Hughes
resides in
Phoenix, Arizona.

These Three Gifts

Because Jesus received gold, frankincense, and myrrh, our children each receive three gifts on Christmas morning. Gifts include something they want (usually a toy), something they need (usually an outfit), and something fun and educational (the parents' choice).

The children's gift lists are well thought out and short, and as parents, we keep from overindulging our children. We have never heard "Is this all there is?" on Christmas morning. Most importantly, all of us keep our focus on Jesus.

Anne Brophy
resides in
Troy, Michigan.

The Family Treasury of Great Holiday Ideas

We have solved the problem of rattling packages and knowing the gift before it's opened. Every year all the gifts to the children have numbers on them, but no names. Mom has a hidden list of what name goes with what number. On Christmas morning the children (right now there are seven still at home) take turns calling off numbers and Mom looks on her list and lets them know who gets what number . . . but no one opens! When all gifts are passed out and stacked in front of each child, Mom tells who should open what number. There is no more paper flying as one gift is opened at a time. Mom even gets to see gifts being opened (as does everyone else) and thank yous get said. After ten years, no one has found Mom's special list!

Sheila Truhlar
resides in
Manhattan, Illinois.

THE PROPER FOCUS

To keep the focus of Christmas on the birth of Jesus, we have always kept the "under the tree" gifts in a separate room of the house. We let our preschooler play with the ornaments on the tree and role-play with the manger scene under the tree. Of course, many of the ornaments end up more on the floor than on the once carefully decorated tree! We bring in the gifts on Christmas Day when we are ready to open them.

Sharon Cofran Skinner
resides in
Pembroke, New Hampshire.

REMEMBER

ONE GIFT

For God so loved the world that he gave His only begotten Son . . . .
(John 3:16)   Since God gave us the gift of His Son, our family
has decided to give only one gift to each other. We focus on the
true holiday message, and we also don't spend as much!

Julie S. Long Civitts
resides in
Toccoa, Georgia.

THE EMPHASIS IS ON GIVING

Before opening gifts on Christmas morning, we arrange all the
presents in piles in front of the person the gift is *from*. Then we
take turns going around the room and each person, one at a
time, gives out the presents they bought. That way there isn't a
lot of confusion at the same time, and you get to see the person
open the present you chose especially for them. It also helps
take the emphasis off *getting*, and puts it back on the *giving*
spirit of Christmas.

Becky S. Shipp
resides in
Flint, Michigan.

n my family, we conclude our Christmas dinner by singing "The Twelve Days of Christmas." Each dinner guest finds their "part" when they sit down as each table setting has a "day of Christmas" glass by it. We have had some wonderful moments s our "choir" sings. Each year we make an audiotape of the ong and now—years later—it is nice to sit back and listen to ur collection and "feel" those voices that no longer grace our arth, yet come home again at Christmas.

Ann Davies
resides in
Valparaiso, Indiana.

TAKE TWO CRANBERRIES

Before Christmas dinner, put two fresh cranberries on each plate. After the family is seated, pass around a basket and, as cranberries are dropped in, share two ways in which Christmas s special to us. Follow by reading John 3:16, and conclude with prayer.*

*Let's Make a Memory, Gloria Gaither and Shirley Dobson, Copyright © 1983, Word, Inc., Dallas, Texas. Used by permission.

REMEMBER

My family decided to embrace Kwanzaa as a family tradition. Kwanzaa means "the first" or "the first fruits of harvest," in the East African language of Kiswahili. The African-American based holiday was founded in 1966 by Dr. Maulana Karenga. Not a substitute for Christmas, Kwanzaa is celebrated from 26 December to 1 January for the seven African principles and precepts that bring a sense of culture and community. The principles are Umoja (Unity), Kujichagulia (Self-Determination), Ujima (Collective Work and Responsibility), Ujamma (Cooperative Economics), Nia (Purpose), Kuumba (Creativity), and Imani (Faith). I want my children to look in the mirror and not be disappointed in being one of God's creation. I know that if they love who they are, they will then be able to love others. We exchange homemade gifts, Afrocentric reading material, or demonstrate a talent by singing a song or reading a poem that celebrates who we are. We all wear a piece of traditional African clothing. We have a potluck with friends and loved ones on the 31 December and everyone brings an ethnic dish.

Diane G. Gardin
resides in
Sierra Vista, Arizona.

AN UNDECORATING PARTY

For years I took down the tree after Christmas all by myself and would feel kind of sad about it. One year my husband suggested we make a party of it and now I look forward to it. We put on Christmas music and I make hot chocolate and popcorn. We drink, eat, and talk as we take the ornaments off the tree. When it is all finished we go out to eat at a favorite restaurant.

Kimberly Miller Wentworth
resides in
Colbert, Georgia.

Everyone Brings
A Covered Dish!

As each guest arrives, they draw a slip assigning
them a specific duty:

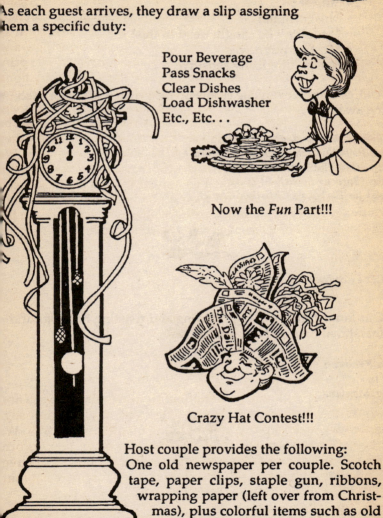

Pour Beverage
Pass Snacks
Clear Dishes
Load Dishwasher
Etc., Etc. . .

Now the *Fun* Part!!!

Crazy Hat Contest!!!

Host couple provides the following:
One old newspaper per couple. Scotch
tape, paper clips, staple gun, ribbons,
wrapping paper (left over from Christmas), plus colorful items such as old
silk flowers and feathers. Place all

REMEMBER

material in center of room and allow thirty minutes for every one to create a millinery masterpiece!

Award prizes for as many categories as you wish:

- Silliest
- Most original
- I wouldn't be caught dead in this!
- Most aerodynamic
- Most ecologically sensitive

And, of course, everyone cleans up their own mess before accepting award.

Hermine and Al Hartley
are the author-illustrator team that created
the best-selling The Family Book of
Manners *(Barbour Books). Al is the*
cartoonist for Barbour's Christian Comic
series.

LET IT SNOW!

Our family enjoys going sledding and roasting hot dogs and marshmallows on New Year's Day.

Glenda Kreiman
resides in
Lindsay, Montana.

The Family Treasury of Great Holiday Ideas

INDEX OF CONTRIBUTORS

The Family Treasury of Great Holiday Ideas

INDEX OF CONTRIBUTORS

K *(continued from previous page)*

(continued from previous page)

INDEX OF CONTRIBUTORS

T

Taylor, Frances M.   184
Truhlar, Sheila   249
Turner, Joyce   17

U

Urban, Gayle B.   128, 146, 154

V

Vetense, Patricia   29, 64

W

Walz, Dana   163
Wentworth, Kimberly M.   205, 241, 252
Werner, Vi   139
White, Diana M.   229
Whitney, Betsy   52
Wiggins, VeraLee   145

Y

Yapp, Kathleen   13

Z

Zeisler, Gloria   115, 117

NOTES

NOTES

NOTES

❧ NOTES ❧